THE VISUAL
DICTIONARY *of the*
UNIVERSE

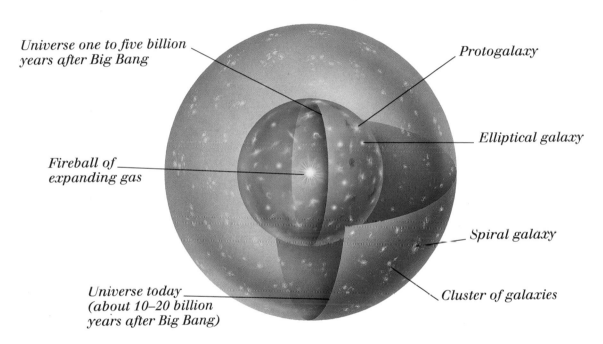

Universe one to five billion
years after Big Bang

Protogalaxy

Fireball of
expanding gas

Elliptical galaxy

Spiral galaxy

Universe today
(about 10–20 billion
years after Big Bang)

Cluster of galaxies

ORIGIN AND EXPANSION OF THE UNIVERSE

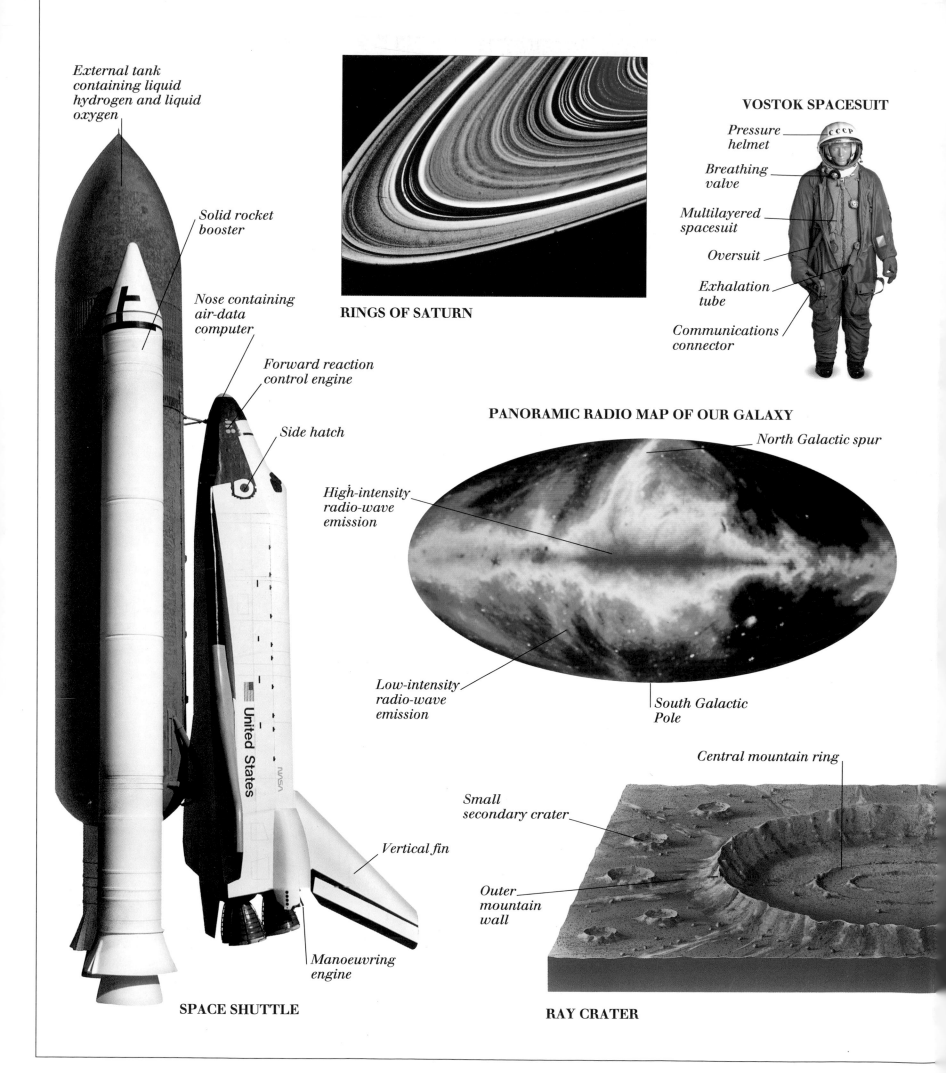

External tank containing liquid hydrogen and liquid oxygen

Solid rocket booster

Nose containing air-data computer

Forward reaction control engine

Side hatch

RINGS OF SATURN

VOSTOK SPACESUIT

Pressure helmet

Breathing valve

Multilayered spacesuit

Oversuit

Exhalation tube

Communications connector

PANORAMIC RADIO MAP OF OUR GALAXY

North Galactic spur

High-intensity radio-wave emission

Low-intensity radio-wave emission

South Galactic Pole

Central mountain ring

Small secondary crater

Outer mountain wall

Vertical fin

Manoeuvring engine

SPACE SHUTTLE

RAY CRATER

THE VISUAL
DICTIONARY *of the*
UNIVERSE

Ascraeus Mons (volcano)

Pavonis Mons (volcano)

Valles Marineris

MARS

Ray of ejecta (ejected material)

Loose ejected rock

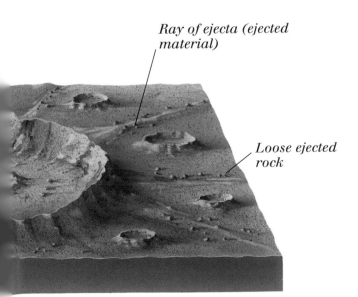

DORLING KINDERSLEY
LONDON • NEW YORK • SYDNEY • MOSCOW

A DORLING KINDERSLEY BOOK

PROJECT ART EDITOR DUNCAN BROWN
DESIGN ASSISTANTS SUSAN KNIGHT, ELLEN WOODWARD

PROJECT EDITOR PAUL DOCHERTY
EDITORIAL ASSISTANT EMILY HILL
ASTRONOMY CONSULTANT EDITOR SUE BECKLAKE
SPACE TECHNOLOGY CONSULTANT EDITOR KENNETH W. GATLAND

MANAGING ART EDITOR PHILIP GILDERDALE
SENIOR EDITOR MARTYN PAGE
MANAGING EDITOR RUTH MIDGLEY

PHOTOGRAPHY ANDY CRAWFORD, BOB GATHANY
ILLUSTRATIONS CHRIS LYON, JULIAN BAUM, RICK BLAKELEY, KUO KANG CHEN, MARK FRANKLIN, SELWYN HUTCHINSON
PRODUCTION JAYNE SIMPSON

Perseus Arm

Nucleus

Crux-Centaurus Arm

Sagittarius Arm

Location of
Solar System

Orion Arm (Local Arm)

OVERHEAD VIEW OF OUR GALAXY

FIRST PUBLISHED IN GREAT BRITAIN IN 1993
BY DORLING KINDERSLEY LIMITED,
9 HENRIETTA STREET, LONDON WC2E 8PS
VISIT US ON THE WORLD WIDE WEB AT
HTTP://WWW.DK.COM
COPYRIGHT © 1993 DORLING KINDERSLEY LIMITED, LONDON
REPRINTED 1994, 1997

A CIP CATALOGUE RECORD FOR THIS BOOK IS AVAILABLE FROM THE BRITISH LIBRARY

ISBN 0 7513 1034 4

REPRODUCED BY COLOURSCAN, SINGAPORE
PRINTED AND BOUND BY ARNOLDO MONDADORI, VERONA, ITALY

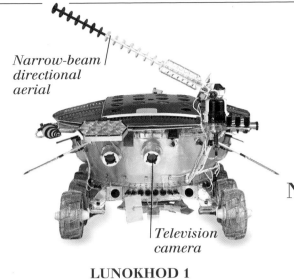

Narrow-beam directional aerial

Television camera

LUNOKHOD 1

Contents

THE UNIVERSE 6

GALAXIES 8

THE MILKY WAY 10

NEBULAE AND STAR CLUSTERS 12

STARS OF NORTHERN SKIES 14

STARS OF SOUTHERN SKIES 16

STARS 18

SMALL STARS 20

MASSIVE STARS 22

NEUTRON STARS AND BLACK HOLES 24

THE SOLAR SYSTEM 26

THE SUN 28

MERCURY 30

VENUS 32

THE EARTH 34

THE MOON 36

MARS 38

JUPITER 40

SATURN 42

URANUS 44

NEPTUNE AND PLUTO 46

ASTEROIDS, COMETS, AND METEOROIDS 48

OBSERVING SPACE 50

MANNED SPACE EXPLORATION 52

LUNAR EXPLORATION 54

ASTRONOMICAL DATA 56

GLOSSARY 59

INDEX 60

ACKNOWLEDGMENTS 64

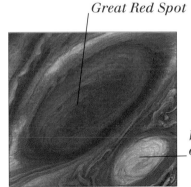

Thin, straight gas tail

Broad, curved dust tail

Coma surrounding nucleus of dust and frozen gases

STRUCTURE OF A COMET

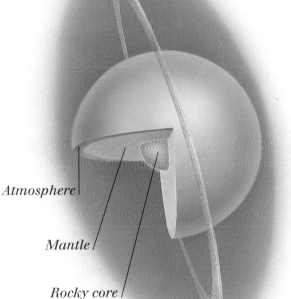

Rings of rocks and dust

Atmosphere

Mantle

Rocky core

URANUS

Great Red Spot

White oval

CLOUD FEATURES OF JUPITER

Stone (olivine)

Iron

STONY-IRON METEORITE

Heat shield

Parachute container

Radiator

High-gain parabolic aerial

Solar panel

MARS 3 ORBITER AND LANDER

The Universe

Fireball of rapidly expanding, extremely hot gas lasting about one million years

THE UNIVERSE CONTAINS EVERYTHING that exists, from the tiniest subatomic particles to galactic superclusters (the largest structures known). Nobody knows how big the Universe is, but astronomers estimate that it contains about 100 billion galaxies, each comprising an average of 100 billion stars. The most widely accepted theory about the origin of the Universe is the Big Bang theory, which states that the Universe came into being in a huge explosion – the Big Bang – that took place between 10 and 20 billion years ago. The Universe initially consisted of a very hot, dense fireball of expanding, cooling gas. After about one million years, the gas probably began to condense into localized clumps called protogalaxies. During the next five billion years, the protogalaxies continued condensing, forming galaxies in which stars were being born. Today, billions of years later, the Universe as a whole is still expanding, although there are localized areas in which objects are held together by gravity; for example, many galaxies are found in clusters. The Big Bang theory is supported by the discovery of faint, cool background radiation coming evenly from all directions. This radiation is believed to be the remnant of the radiation produced by the Big Bang. Small "ripples" in the temperature of the cosmic background radiation are thought to be evidence of slight fluctuations in the density of the early Universe, which resulted in the formation of galaxies. Astronomers do not yet know if the Universe is "closed", which means it will eventually stop expanding and begin to contract, or if it is "open", which means it will continue expanding forever.

FALSE-COLOUR MICROWAVE MAP OF COSMIC BACKGROUND RADIATION

Pink indicates "warm ripples" in background radiation

Pale blue indicates "cool ripples" in background radiation

Deep blue indicates background radiation corresponding to -270.3°C (remnant of the Big Bang)

Low-energy microwave radiation corresponding to about -270°C

Red and pink band indicates radiation from our galaxy

High-energy gamma radiation corresponding to about 3,000°C

6

ORIGIN AND EXPANSION OF THE UNIVERSE

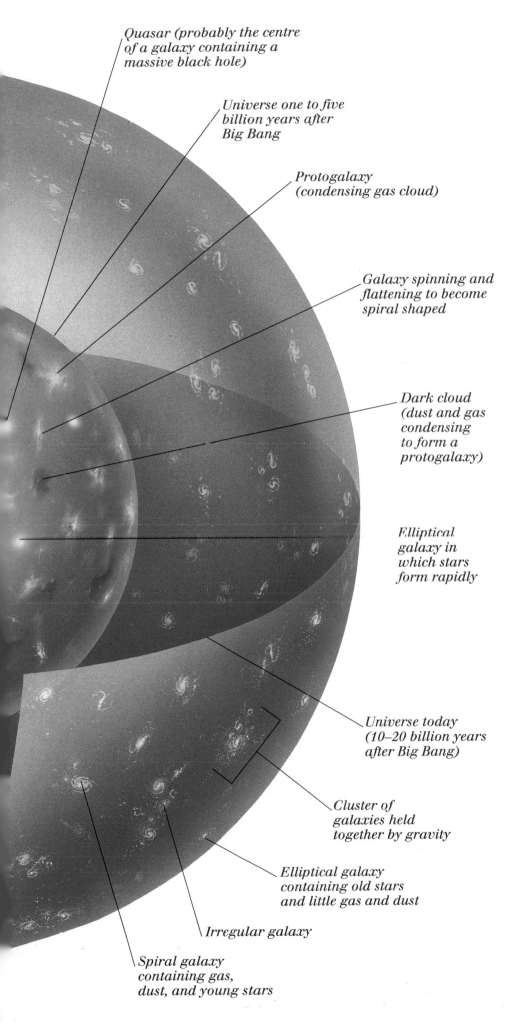

Quasar (probably the centre
of a galaxy containing a
massive black hole)

Universe one to five
billion years after
Big Bang

Protogalaxy
(condensing gas cloud)

Galaxy spinning and
flattening to become
spiral shaped

Dark cloud
(dust and gas
condensing
to form a
protogalaxy)

Elliptical
galaxy in
which stars
form rapidly

Universe today
(10–20 billion years
after Big Bang)

Cluster of
galaxies held
together by gravity

Elliptical galaxy
containing old stars
and little gas and dust

Irregular galaxy

Spiral galaxy
containing gas,
dust, and young stars

OBJECTS IN THE UNIVERSE

**CLUSTER OF
GALAXIES IN VIRGO**

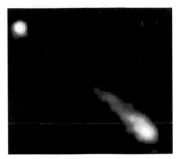

**FALSE-COLOUR IMAGE
OF 3C273 (QUASAR)**

**NGC 4406
(ELLIPTICAL GALAXY)**

**NGC 5236
(SPIRAL GALAXY)**

**NGC 6822
(IRREGULAR GALAXY)**

**THE ROSETTE NEBULA
(EMISSION NEBULA)**

**THE JEWEL BOX
(STAR CLUSTER)**

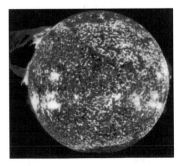

**THE SUN
(MAIN SEQUENCE STAR)**

EARTH

THE MOON

Galaxies

SOMBRERO,
A SPIRAL GALAXY

A GALAXY IS A HUGE MASS OF STARS, nebulae, and interstellar material. The smallest galaxies contain about 100,000 stars, while the largest contain up to 3,000 billion stars. There are three main types of galaxy, classified according to their shape: elliptical, which are oval shaped; spiral, which have arms spiralling outwards from a central bulge; and irregular, which have no obvious shape. Sometimes, the shape of a galaxy is distorted by a collision with another galaxy. Quasars (quasi-stellar objects) are thought to be galactic nuclei but are so far away that their exact nature is still uncertain. They are compact, highly luminous objects in the outer reaches of the known Universe: while the furthest known "ordinary" galaxies are about 10 billion light years away, the furthest known quasar is about 15 billion light years away. Active galaxies, such as Seyfert galaxies and radio galaxies, emit intense radiation. In a Seyfert galaxy, this radiation comes from the galactic nucleus; in a radio galaxy, it also comes from huge lobes on either side of the galaxy. The radiation from active galaxies and quasars is thought to be caused by black holes (see pp. 24-25).

OPTICAL IMAGE OF NGC 4486 (ELLIPTICAL GALAXY)

Globular cluster containing very old red giants

Central region containing old red giants

Less densely populated region

Neighbouring galaxy

OPTICAL IMAGE OF LARGE MAGELLANIC CLOUD (IRREGULAR GALAXY)

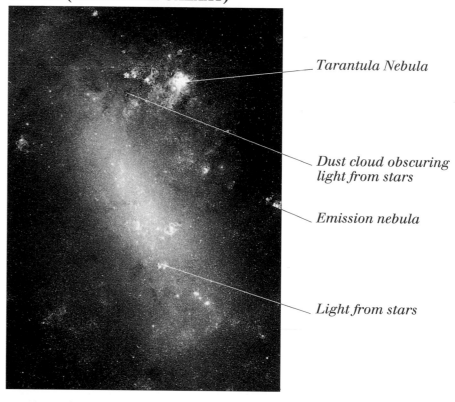

Tarantula Nebula

Dust cloud obscuring light from stars

Emission nebula

Light from stars

OPTICAL IMAGE OF NGC 2997 (SPIRAL GALAXY)

Glowing nebula in spiral arm

Spiral arm containing young stars

Galactic nucleus containing old stars

Dust in spiral arm reflecting blue light from hot young stars

Hot, ionized hydrogen gas emitting red light

Dust lane

OPTICAL IMAGE OF CENTAURUS A (RADIO GALAXY)

Dust lane crossing elliptical galaxy

Galactic nucleus containing powerful source of radiation

Light from old stars

FALSE-COLOUR RADIO IMAGE OF CENTAURUS A

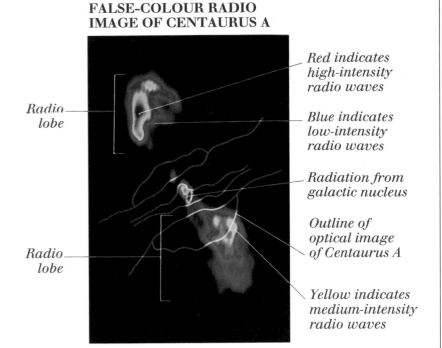

Red indicates high-intensity radio waves

Blue indicates low-intensity radio waves

Radiation from galactic nucleus

Outline of optical image of Centaurus A

Yellow indicates medium-intensity radio waves

Radio lobe

Radio lobe

FALSE-COLOUR RADIO IMAGE OF 3C273 (QUASAR)

Radiation from jet of high-energy particles moving away from quasar

Blue indicates low-intensity radio waves

Quasar nucleus

White indicates high-intensity radio waves

OPTICAL IMAGE OF NGC 1566 (SEYFERT GALAXY)

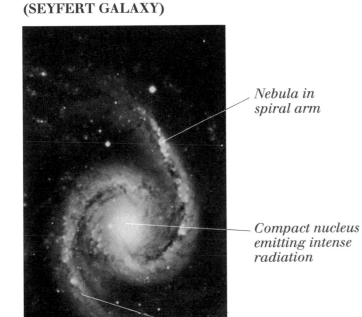

Nebula in spiral arm

Compact nucleus emitting intense radiation

Spiral arm

FALSE-COLOUR OPTICAL IMAGE OF NGC 5754 (TWO COLLIDING GALAXIES)

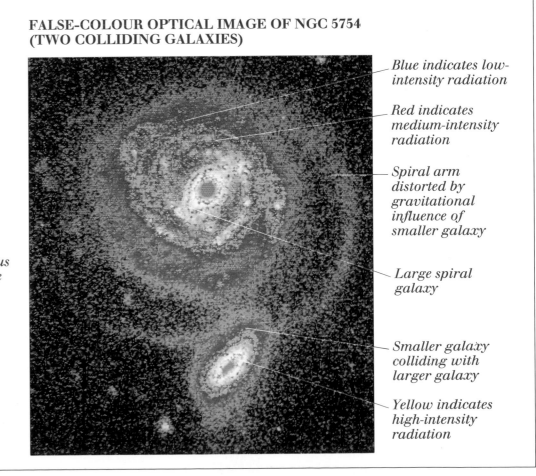

Blue indicates low-intensity radiation

Red indicates medium-intensity radiation

Spiral arm distorted by gravitational influence of smaller galaxy

Large spiral galaxy

Smaller galaxy colliding with larger galaxy

Yellow indicates high-intensity radiation

The Milky Way

VIEW TOWARDS GALACTIC CENTRE

THE MILKY WAY IS THE NAME GIVEN TO THE FAINT BAND OF LIGHT that stretches across the night sky. This light comes from stars and nebulae in our galaxy, known as the Milky Way Galaxy or simply as "the Galaxy". The Galaxy is shaped like a spiral, with a dense central bulge that is encircled by four arms spiralling outwards and surrounded by a less dense halo. We cannot see the spiral shape because the Solar System is in one of the spiral arms, the Orion Arm (also called the Local Arm). From our position, the centre of the Galaxy is completely obscured by dust clouds; as a result, optical maps give only a limited view of the Galaxy. However, a more complete picture can be obtained by studying radio, infra-red, and other radiation. The central bulge of the Galaxy is a relatively small, dense sphere that contains mainly older red and yellow stars. The halo is a less dense region in which the oldest stars are situated; some of these stars may be as old as the Galaxy itself (possibly 15 billion years). The spiral arms contain mainly hot, young, blue stars, as well as nebulae (clouds of dust and gas inside which stars are born). The Galaxy is vast, about 100,000 light years across (a light year is about 9,460 billion kilometres); in comparison, the Solar System seems small, at about 12 light hours across (about 13 billion kilometres). The entire Galaxy is rotating in space, although the inner stars travel faster than those further out. The Sun, which is about two-thirds out from the centre, completes one lap of the Galaxy about every 220 million years.

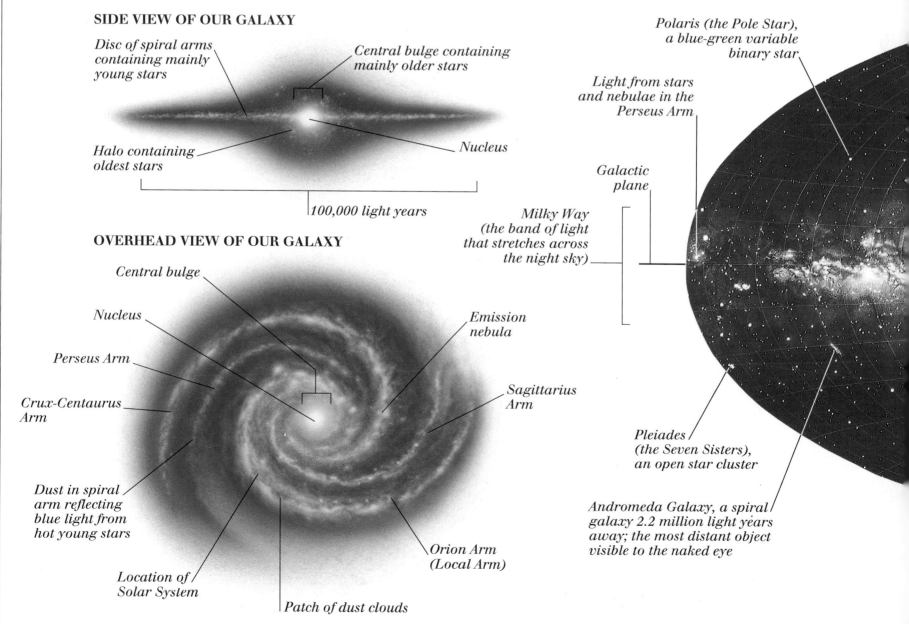

SIDE VIEW OF OUR GALAXY

Disc of spiral arms containing mainly young stars

Central bulge containing mainly older stars

Halo containing oldest stars

Nucleus

100,000 light years

OVERHEAD VIEW OF OUR GALAXY

Central bulge

Nucleus

Perseus Arm

Crux-Centaurus Arm

Dust in spiral arm reflecting blue light from hot young stars

Location of Solar System

Patch of dust clouds

Emission nebula

Sagittarius Arm

Orion Arm (Local Arm)

PANORAMIC OPTICAL MAP OF OUR GALAXY AND NEARBY GALAXIES

Polaris (the Pole Star), a blue-green variable binary star

Light from stars and nebulae in the Perseus Arm

Galactic plane

Milky Way (the band of light that stretches across the night sky)

Pleiades (the Seven Sisters), an open star cluster

Andromeda Galaxy, a spiral galaxy 2.2 million light years away; the most distant object visible to the naked eye

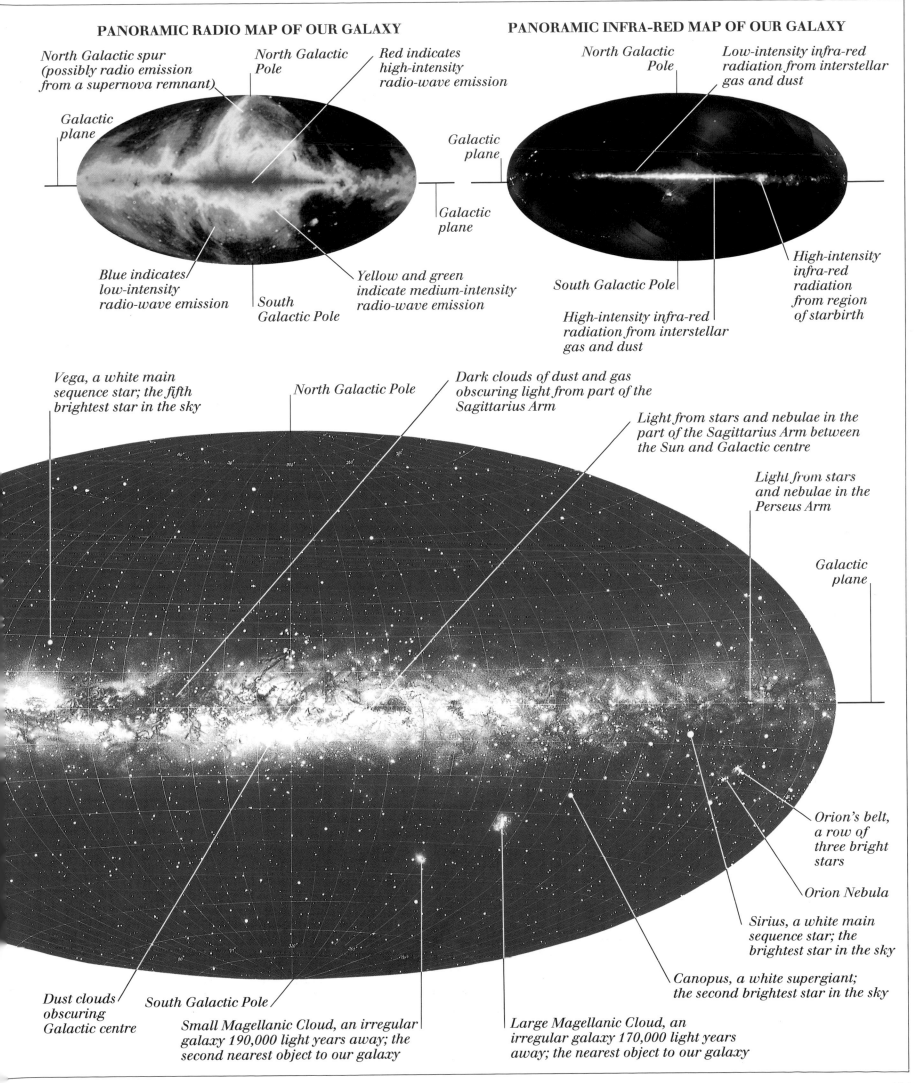

PANORAMIC RADIO MAP OF OUR GALAXY

North Galactic spur
(possibly radio emission
from a supernova remnant)

North Galactic
Pole

Red indicates
high-intensity
radio-wave emission

Galactic
plane

Blue indicates
low-intensity
radio-wave emission

South
Galactic Pole

Yellow and green
indicate medium-intensity
radio-wave emission

PANORAMIC INFRA-RED MAP OF OUR GALAXY

North Galactic
Pole

Low-intensity infra-red
radiation from interstellar
gas and dust

Galactic
plane

Galactic
plane

South Galactic Pole

High-intensity
infra-red
radiation
from region
of starbirth

High-intensity infra-red
radiation from interstellar
gas and dust

Vega, a white main
sequence star; the fifth
brightest star in the sky

North Galactic Pole

Dark clouds of dust and gas
obscuring light from part of the
Sagittarius Arm

Light from stars and nebulae in the
part of the Sagittarius Arm between
the Sun and Galactic centre

Light from stars
and nebulae in the
Perseus Arm

Galactic
plane

Orion's belt,
a row of
three bright
stars

Orion Nebula

Sirius, a white main
sequence star; the
brightest star in the sky

Canopus, a white supergiant;
the second brightest star in the sky

Dust clouds
obscuring
Galactic centre

South Galactic Pole

Small Magellanic Cloud, an irregular
galaxy 190,000 light years away; the
second nearest object to our galaxy

Large Magellanic Cloud, an
irregular galaxy 170,000 light years
away; the nearest object to our galaxy

Nebulae and star clusters

HODGE 11, A GLOBULAR CLUSTER

A NEBULA IS A CLOUD OF DUST AND GAS inside a galaxy. Nebulae become visible if the gas glows, or if the cloud reflects starlight or obscures light from more distant objects. Emission nebulae shine because their gas emits light when it is stimulated by radiation from hot young stars. Reflection nebulae shine because their dust reflects light from stars in or around the nebula. Dark nebulae appear as silhouettes because they block out light from shining nebulae or stars behind them. Two types of nebula are associated with dying stars: planetary nebulae and supernova remnants. Both consist of expanding shells of gas that were once the outer layers of a star. A planetary nebula is a gas shell drifting away from a dying stellar core. A supernova remnant is a gas shell moving away from a stellar core at great speed following a violent explosion called a supernova (see pp. 22-23). Stars are often found in groups known as clusters. Open clusters are loose groups of a few thousand young stars that were born in the same cloud and are drifting apart. Globular clusters are densely packed, roughly spherical groups of hundreds of thousands of older stars.

TRIFID NEBULA (EMISSION NEBULA)

Reflection nebula

Emission nebula

Dust lane

Starbirth region (area in which dust and gas clump together to form stars)

PLEIADES (OPEN STAR CLUSTER) WITH A REFLECTION NEBULA

Wisps of dust and hydrogen gas remaining from cloud in which stars formed

Young star in an open cluster of 300–500 stars

Reflection nebula

HORSEHEAD NEBULA (DARK NEBULA)

Glowing filament of hot, ionized hydrogen gas

Alnitak (star in Orion's belt)

Dust lane

Emission nebula

Star near southern end of Orion's belt

Emission nebula

Horsehead Nebula

Reflection nebula

Dark nebula obscuring light from distant stars

ORION NEBULA (DIFFUSE EMISSION NEBULA)

Glowing cloud of dust and hydrogen gas forming part of Orion Nebula

Dust cloud

Trapezium (group of four young stars)

Red light from hot, ionized hydrogen gas

Gas cloud emitting light due to ultraviolet radiation from the four young Trapezium stars

Green light from hot, ionized oxygen gas

Glowing filament of hot, ionized hydrogen gas

HELIX NEBULA (PLANETARY NEBULA)

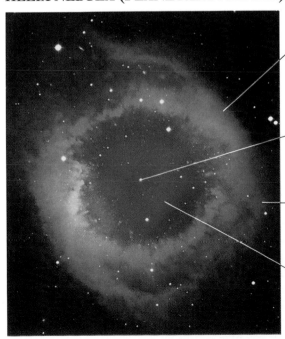

Planetary nebula (gas shell expanding outwards from dying stellar core)

Stellar core at a temperature of about 100,000°C

Red light from hot, ionized hydrogen gas

Blue-green light from hot, ionized oxygen and nitrogen gases

VELA SUPERNOVA REMNANT

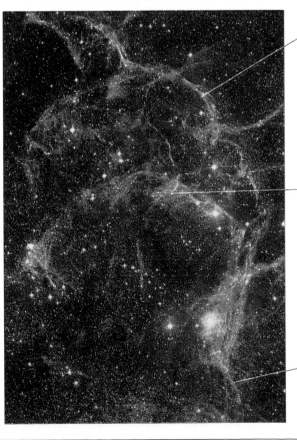

Supernova remnant (gas shell consisting of outer layers of star thrown off in supernova explosion)

Hydrogen gas emitting red light due to being heated by supernova explosion

Glowing filament of hot, ionized hydrogen gas

Stars of northern skies

WHEN YOU LOOK AT THE NORTHERN SKY, you look away from the densely populated Galactic centre, so the northern sky generally appears less bright than the southern sky (see pp. 16-17). Among the best-known sights in the northern sky are the constellations Ursa Major (the Great Bear) and Orion. Some ancient civilizations believed that the stars were fixed to a celestial sphere surrounding the Earth, and modern maps of the sky are based on a similar idea. The North and South Poles of this imaginary celestial sphere are directly above the North and South Poles of the Earth, at the points where the Earth's axis of rotation intersects the sphere. The celestial North Pole is at the centre of the map shown here, and Polaris (the Pole Star) lies very close to it. The celestial equator marks a projection of the Earth's equator on the sphere. The ecliptic marks the path of the Sun across the sky as the Earth orbits the Sun. The Moon and planets move against the background of the stars because the stars are much more distant; the nearest star outside the Solar System (Proxima Centauri) is more than 50,000 times further away than the planet Jupiter.

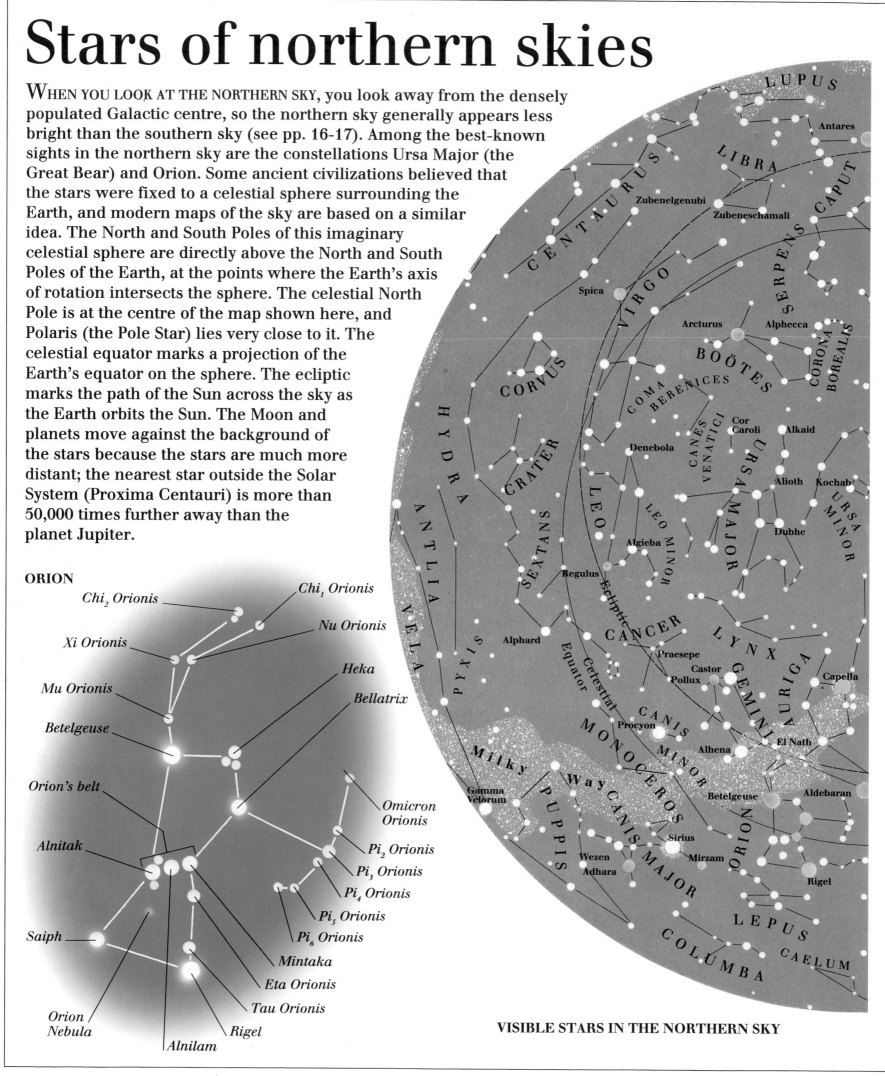

ORION

VISIBLE STARS IN THE NORTHERN SKY

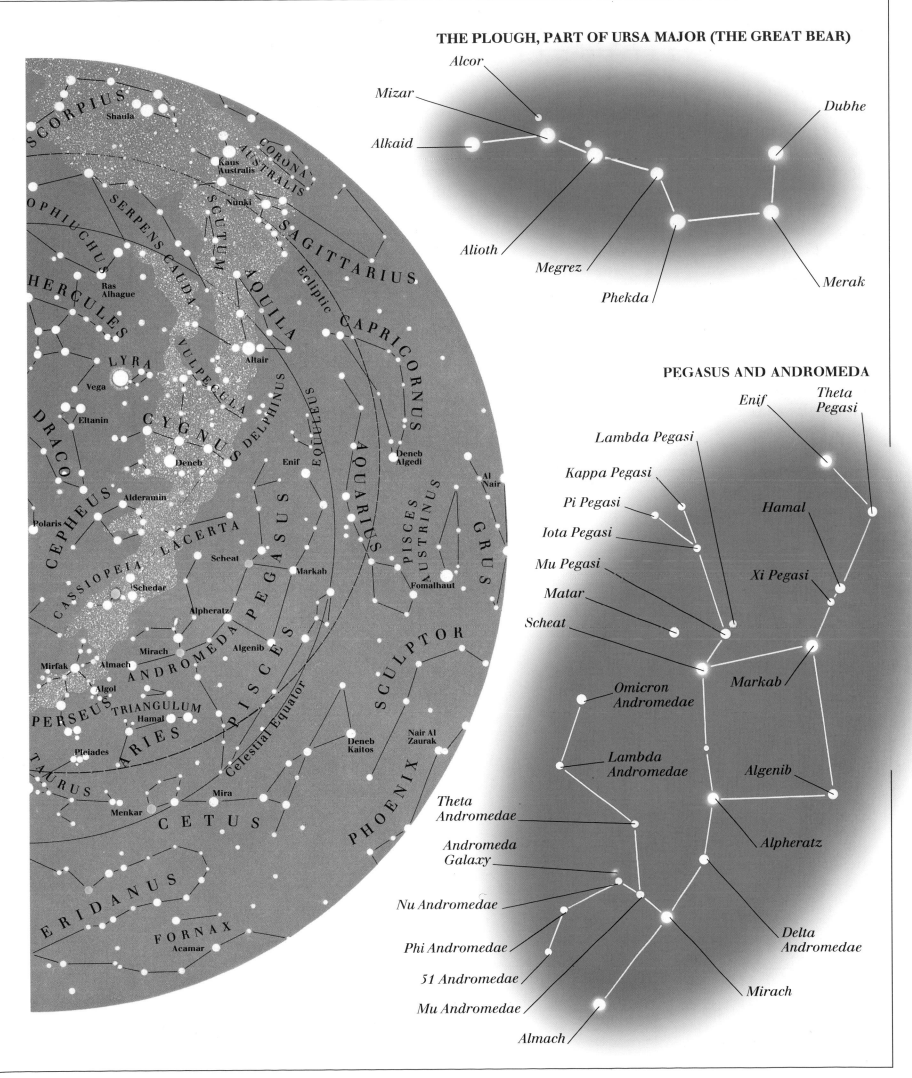

THE PLOUGH, PART OF URSA MAJOR (THE GREAT BEAR)

Alcor
Mizar
Dubhe
Alkaid
Alioth
Megrez
Merak
Phekda

PEGASUS AND ANDROMEDA

Enif
Theta Pegasi
Lambda Pegasi
Kappa Pegasi
Hamal
Pi Pegasi
Iota Pegasi
Xi Pegasi
Mu Pegasi
Matar
Scheat
Markab
Omicron Andromedae
Lambda Andromedae
Algenib
Theta Andromedae
Alpheratz
Andromeda Galaxy
Nu Andromedae
Delta Andromedae
Phi Andromedae
51 Andromedae
Mu Andromedae
Mirach
Almach

SCORPIUS
Shaula
CORONA AUSTRALIS
Kaus Australis
SERPENS CAUDA
Nunki
SCUTUM
SAGITTARIUS
OPHIUCHUS
Ras Alhague
AQUILA
Ecliptic
HERCULES
Altair
CAPRICORNUS
LYRA
Vega
VULPECULA
DELPHINUS
Eltanin
CYGNUS
EQUULEUS
AQUARIUS
DRACO
Deneb
Enif
Deneb Algedi
Alderamin
PISCES AUSTRINUS
Al Nair
CEPHEUS
LACERTA
Polaris
Scheat
PEGASUS
Markab
GRUS
CASSIOPEIA
Schedar
Fomalhaut
Alpheratz
ANDROMEDA
Mirach
Algenib
SCULPTOR
Mirfak
Almach
PISCES
Algol
PERSEUS
TRIANGULUM
Hamal
ARIES
Celestial Equator
Deneb Kaitos
Nair Al Zaurak
Pleiades
TAURUS
Mira
PHOENIX
Menkar
CETUS
ERIDANUS
FORNAX
Acamar

15

Stars of southern skies

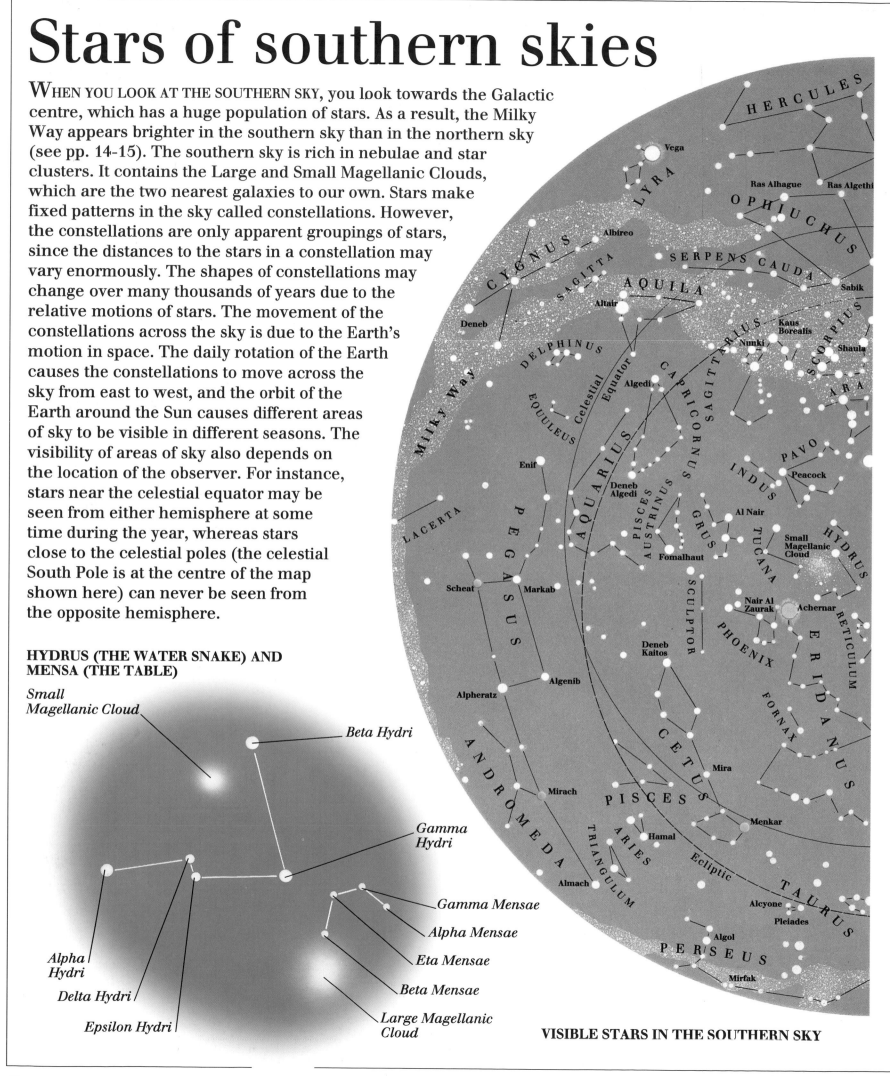

WHEN YOU LOOK AT THE SOUTHERN SKY, you look towards the Galactic centre, which has a huge population of stars. As a result, the Milky Way appears brighter in the southern sky than in the northern sky (see pp. 14-15). The southern sky is rich in nebulae and star clusters. It contains the Large and Small Magellanic Clouds, which are the two nearest galaxies to our own. Stars make fixed patterns in the sky called constellations. However, the constellations are only apparent groupings of stars, since the distances to the stars in a constellation may vary enormously. The shapes of constellations may change over many thousands of years due to the relative motions of stars. The movement of the constellations across the sky is due to the Earth's motion in space. The daily rotation of the Earth causes the constellations to move across the sky from east to west, and the orbit of the Earth around the Sun causes different areas of sky to be visible in different seasons. The visibility of areas of sky also depends on the location of the observer. For instance, stars near the celestial equator may be seen from either hemisphere at some time during the year, whereas stars close to the celestial poles (the celestial South Pole is at the centre of the map shown here) can never be seen from the opposite hemisphere.

HYDRUS (THE WATER SNAKE) AND MENSA (THE TABLE)

Small Magellanic Cloud

Beta Hydri

Gamma Hydri

Gamma Mensae

Alpha Mensae

Eta Mensae

Beta Mensae

Alpha Hydri

Delta Hydri

Epsilon Hydri

Large Magellanic Cloud

VISIBLE STARS IN THE SOUTHERN SKY

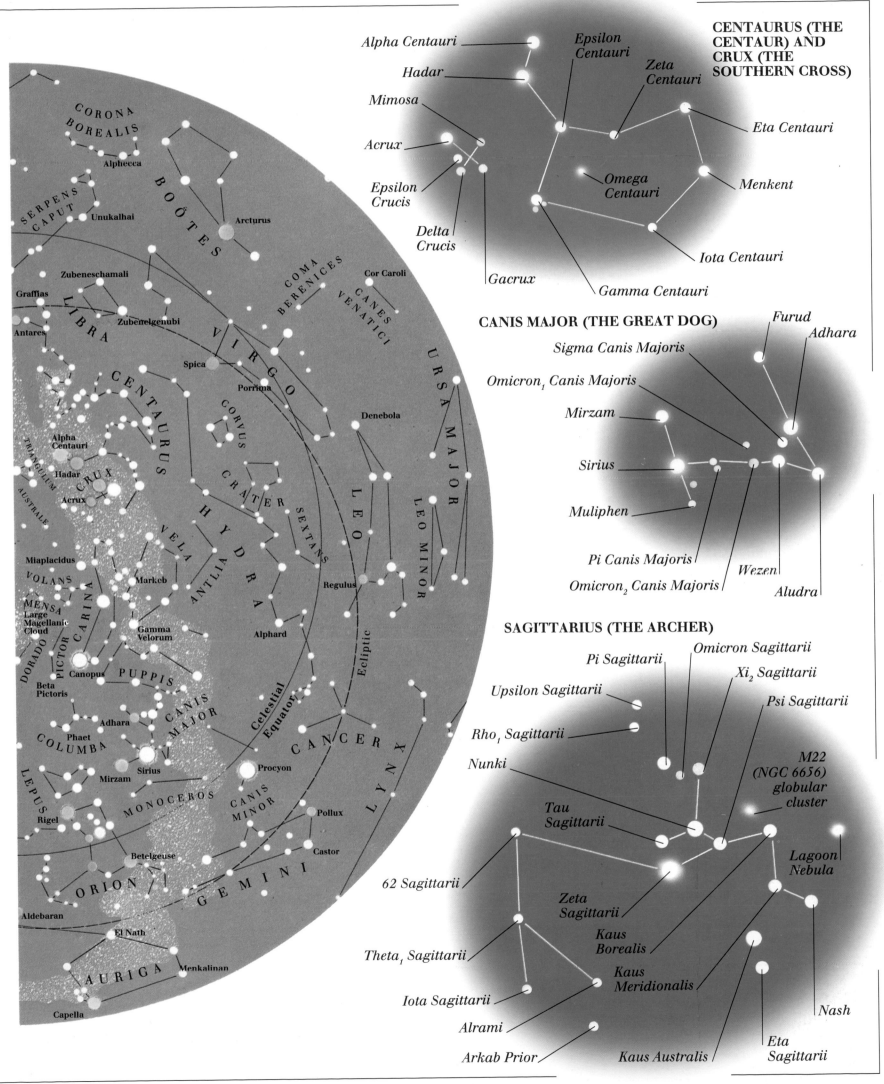

CENTAURUS (THE CENTAUR) AND CRUX (THE SOUTHERN CROSS)

Alpha Centauri
Epsilon Centauri
Hadar
Zeta Centauri
Mimosa
Eta Centauri
Acrux
Epsilon Crucis
Omega Centauri
Menkent
Delta Crucis
Iota Centauri
Gacrux
Gamma Centauri

CANIS MAJOR (THE GREAT DOG)

Furud
Adhara
Sigma Canis Majoris
Omicron₁ Canis Majoris
Mirzam
Sirius
Muliphen
Pi Canis Majoris
Wezen
Omicron₂ Canis Majoris
Aludra

SAGITTARIUS (THE ARCHER)

Omicron Sagittarii
Pi Sagittarii
Xi₂ Sagittarii
Upsilon Sagittarii
Psi Sagittarii
Rho₁ Sagittarii
Nunki
M22 (NGC 6656) globular cluster
Tau Sagittarii
Lagoon Nebula
62 Sagittarii
Zeta Sagittarii
Kaus Borealis
Theta₁ Sagittarii
Kaus Meridionalis
Iota Sagittarii
Nash
Alrami
Eta Sagittarii
Arkab Prior
Kaus Australis

CORONA BOREALIS
Alphecca
SERPENS CAPUT
BOÖTES
Unukalhai
Arcturus
COMA BERENICES
Cor Caroli
CANES VENATICI
Zubeneschamali
Graffias
VIRGO
Antares
LIBRA
Zubenelgenubi
URSA MAJOR
Spica
Porrima
Denebola
CENTAURUS
Alpha Centauri
CORVUS
CRATER
SEXTANS
LEO
LEO MINOR
Hadar
Acrux
HYDRA
Miaplacidus
VELA
ANTLIA
Regulus
VOLANS
Markeb
Alphard
MENSA
Large Magellanic Cloud
CARINA
Gamma Velorum
Ecliptic
DORADO
PICTOR
Canopus
PUPPIS
Celestial Equator
CANCER
Beta Pictoris
CANIS MAJOR
LYNX
COLUMBA
Adhara
Procyon
Phaet
Sirius
CANIS MINOR
Pollux
LEPUS
Mirzam
MONOCEROS
Castor
Rigel
Betelgeuse
GEMINI
ORION
Aldebaran
El Nath
AURIGA
Menkalinan
Capella
TRIANGULUM AUSTRALE
CRUX

Stars

STARS ARE BODIES of hot, glowing gas that are born in nebulae (see pp. 20-23). They vary enormously in size, mass, and temperature: diameters range from about 450 times smaller to over 1,000 times bigger than that of the Sun; masses range from about a twentieth to over 50 solar masses; and surface temperatures range from about 3,000°C to over 50,000°C. The colour of a star is determined by its temperature: the hottest stars are blue and the coolest are red. The Sun, with a surface temperature of 5,500°C, is between these extremes and appears yellow. The energy emitted by a shining star is produced by nuclear fusion in the star's core. The brightness of a star is measured in magnitudes – the brighter the star, the lower its magnitude. There are two types of magnitude: apparent magnitude, which is the brightness seen from Earth, and absolute magnitude, which is the brightness that would be seen from a standard distance of 10 parsecs (32.6 light years). The light emitted by a star may be split to form a spectrum containing a series of dark lines (absorption lines). The patterns of lines indicate the presence of particular chemical elements, enabling astronomers to deduce the composition of the star's atmosphere. The magnitude and spectral type (colour) of stars may be plotted on a graph called a Hertzsprung-Russell diagram, which shows that stars tend to fall into several well-defined groups. The principal groups are main sequence stars (those which are fusing hydrogen to form helium), giants, supergiants, and white dwarfs.

OPEN STAR CLUSTER AND DUST CLOUD

STAR SIZES

Red giant (diameters between about 15 million and 150 million km)

The Sun (main sequence star with diameter about 1.4 million km)

White dwarf (diameters between about 3,000 and 50,000 km)

ENERGY EMISSION FROM THE SUN

Nuclear fusion in core produces gamma rays and neutrinos

Neutrinos travel to Earth directly from Sun's core in about 8 minutes

Lower-energy radiation travels to Earth in about 8 minutes

Earth

Sun

Lower-energy radiation (mainly ultraviolet, infra-red, and light rays) leaves surface

High-energy radiation (gamma rays) loses energy while travelling to surface over 2 million years

STAR MAGNITUDES

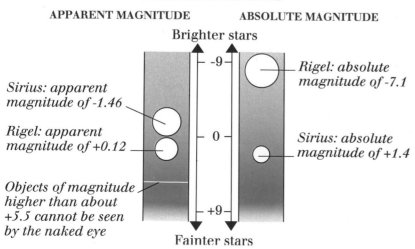

APPARENT MAGNITUDE

ABSOLUTE MAGNITUDE

Brighter stars

-9

0

+9

Fainter stars

Sirius: apparent magnitude of -1.46

Rigel: apparent magnitude of +0.12

Objects of magnitude higher than about +5.5 cannot be seen by the naked eye

Rigel: absolute magnitude of -7.1

Sirius: absolute magnitude of +1.4

NUCLEAR FUSION IN MAIN SEQUENCE STARS LIKE THE SUN

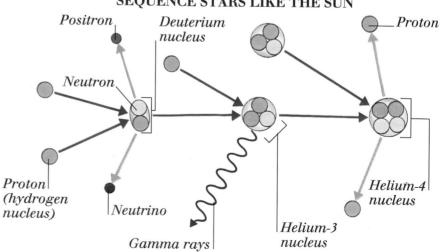

Positron

Deuterium nucleus

Proton

Neutron

Proton (hydrogen nucleus)

Neutrino

Gamma rays

Helium-3 nucleus

Helium-4 nucleus

HERTZSPRUNG-RUSSELL DIAGRAM

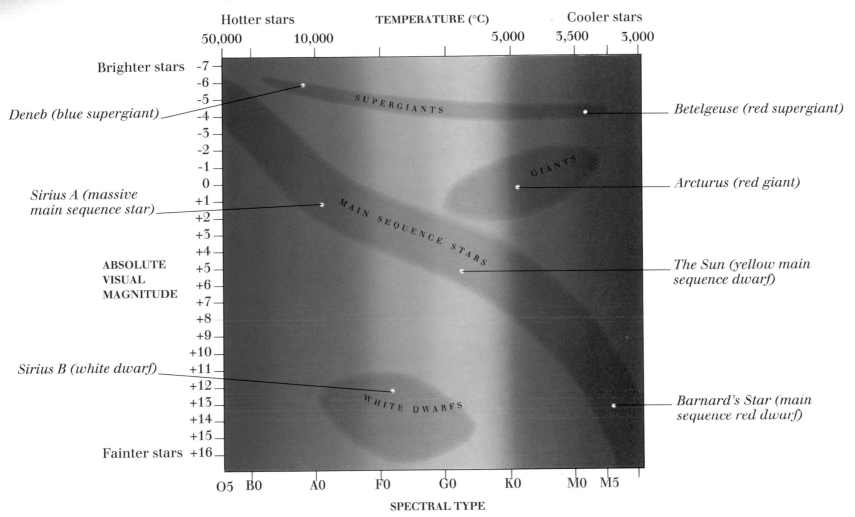

Hotter stars   TEMPERATURE (°C)   Cooler stars

50,000   10,000   5,000   3,500   3,000

Brighter stars

Deneb (blue supergiant)

SUPERGIANTS

Betelgeuse (red supergiant)

GIANTS

Arcturus (red giant)

Sirius A (massive main sequence star)

MAIN SEQUENCE STARS

ABSOLUTE VISUAL MAGNITUDE

The Sun (yellow main sequence dwarf)

Sirius B (white dwarf)

WHITE DWARFS

Barnard's Star (main sequence red dwarf)

Fainter stars

O5   B0   A0   F0   G0   K0   M0   M5

SPECTRAL TYPE

STELLAR SPECTRAL ABSORPTION LINES

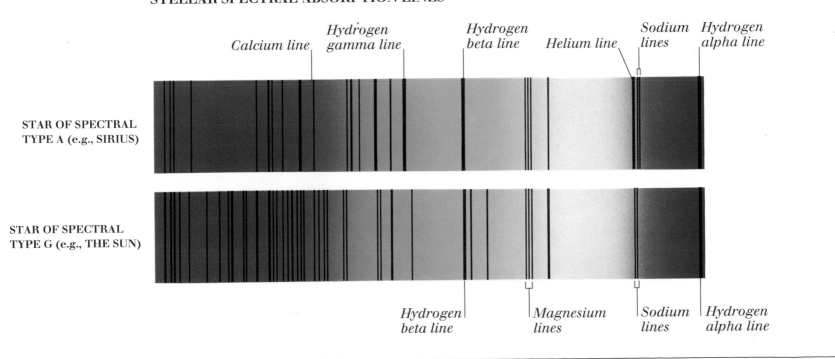

Calcium line   Hydrogen gamma line   Hydrogen beta line   Helium line   Sodium lines   Hydrogen alpha line

STAR OF SPECTRAL TYPE A (e.g., SIRIUS)

STAR OF SPECTRAL TYPE G (e.g., THE SUN)

Hydrogen beta line   Magnesium lines   Sodium lines   Hydrogen alpha line

Small stars

SMALL STARS HAVE A MASS of up to about one and a half times that of the Sun. They begin to form when a region of higher density in a nebula condenses into a huge globule of gas and dust that contracts under its own gravity. Within a globule, regions of condensing matter heat up and begin to glow, forming protostars. If a protostar contains enough matter, the central temperature reaches about 15 million °C. At this temperature, nuclear reactions in which hydrogen fuses to form helium can start. This process releases energy, which prevents the star from contracting further and also causes it to shine; it is now a main sequence star. A star of about one solar mass remains in the main sequence for about 10 billion years, until the hydrogen in the star's core has been converted into helium. The helium core then contracts again, and nuclear reactions continue in a shell around the core. The core becomes hot enough for helium to fuse to form carbon, while the outer layers of the star expand, cool, and shine less brightly. The expanding star is known as a red giant. When the helium in the core runs out, the outer layers of the star may drift off as an expanding gas shell called a planetary nebula. The remaining core (about 80 per cent of the original star) is now in its final stages. It becomes a white dwarf star that gradually cools and dims. When it finally stops shining altogether, the dead star will become a black dwarf.

REGION OF STAR FORMATION IN ORION

STRUCTURE OF A MAIN SEQUENCE STAR

Core containing hydrogen fusing to form helium

Radiative zone

Convective zone

Surface temperature about 5,500°C

Core temperature about 15 million °C

STRUCTURE OF A NEBULA

Young main sequence star

Dense region of dust and gas (mainly hydrogen) condensing under gravity to form globules

Hot, ionized hydrogen gas emitting red light due to being stimulated by radiation from hot young stars

Dark globule of dust and gas (mainly hydrogen) contracting to form protostars

LIFE OF A SMALL STAR OF ABOUT ONE SOLAR MASS

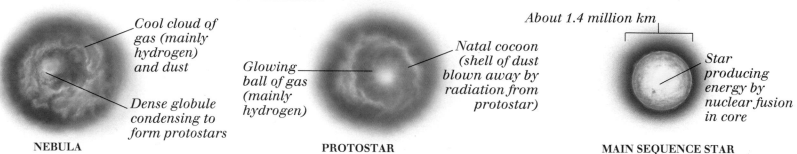

Cool cloud of gas (mainly hydrogen) and dust

Dense globule condensing to form protostars

NEBULA

Glowing ball of gas (mainly hydrogen)

Natal cocoon (shell of dust blown away by radiation from protostar)

PROTOSTAR
Duration: 50 million years

About 1.4 million km

Star producing energy by nuclear fusion in core

MAIN SEQUENCE STAR
Duration: 10 billion years

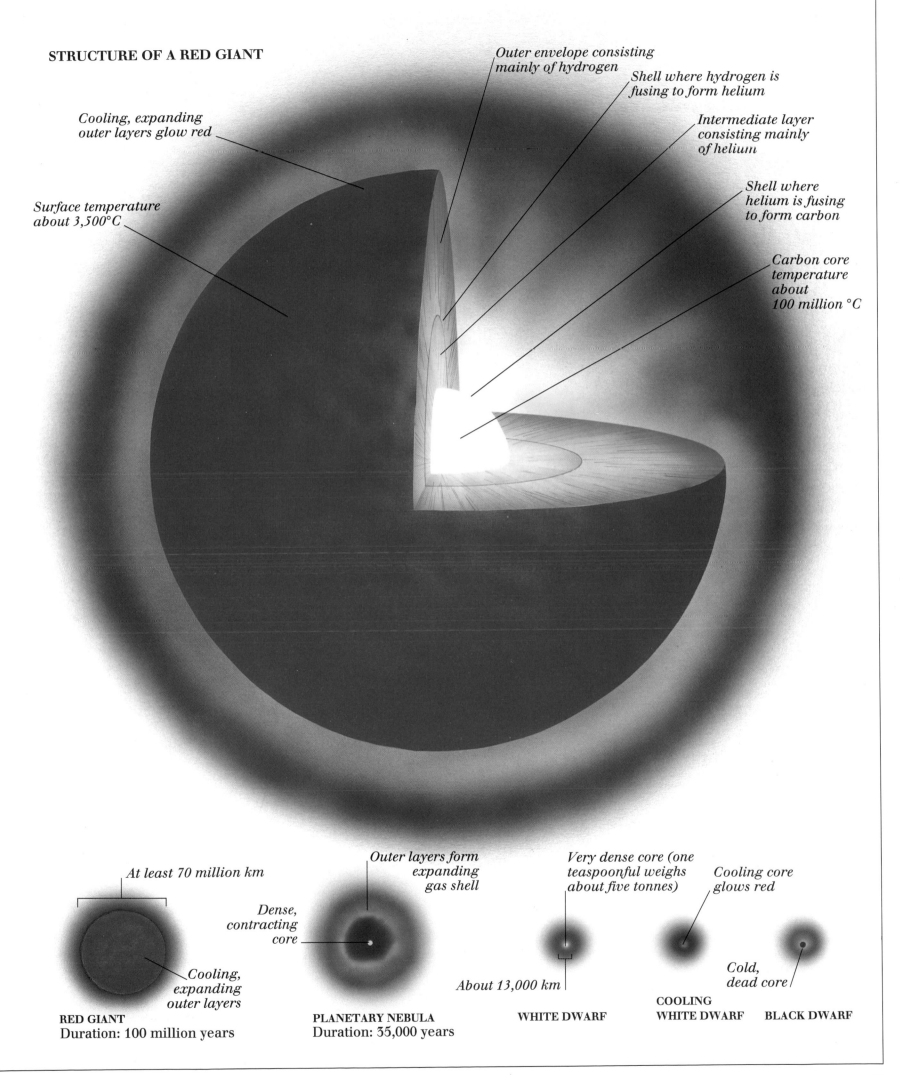

STRUCTURE OF A RED GIANT

Outer envelope consisting mainly of hydrogen

Shell where hydrogen is fusing to form helium

Intermediate layer consisting mainly of helium

Shell where helium is fusing to form carbon

Carbon core temperature about 100 million °C

Cooling, expanding outer layers glow red

Surface temperature about 3,500°C

At least 70 million km

Cooling, expanding outer layers

RED GIANT
Duration: 100 million years

Outer layers form expanding gas shell

Dense, contracting core

PLANETARY NEBULA
Duration: 35,000 years

Very dense core (one teaspoonful weighs about five tonnes)

About 13,000 km

WHITE DWARF

Cooling core glows red

COOLING WHITE DWARF

Cold, dead core

BLACK DWARF

Massive stars

MASSIVE STARS HAVE A MASS AT LEAST THREE TIMES that of the Sun, and some stars are as massive as about 50 Suns. A massive star evolves in a similar way to a small star until it reaches the main sequence stage (see pp. 20-21). During the main sequence, a star shines steadily until the hydrogen in its core has fused to form helium. This process takes billions of years in a small star, but only millions of years in a massive star. A massive star then becomes a red supergiant, which initially consists of a helium core surrounded by outer layers of cooling, expanding gas. Over the next few million years, a series of nuclear reactions form different elements in shells around an iron core. The core eventually collapses in less than a second, causing a massive explosion called a supernova, in which a shock wave blows away the outer layers of the star. Supernovae shine brighter than an entire galaxy for a short time. Sometimes, the core survives the supernova explosion. If the surviving core is between about one and a half and three solar masses, it contracts to become a tiny, dense neutron star. If the core is considerably greater than three solar masses, it contracts to become a black hole (see pp. 24-25).

SUPERNOVA

TARANTULA NEBULA BEFORE SUPERNOVA

STRUCTURE OF A RED SUPERGIANT

Outer envelope consisting mainly of hydrogen

Layer consisting mainly of helium

Layer consisting mainly of carbon

Layer consisting mainly of oxygen

Layer consisting mainly of silicon

Shell of hydrogen fusing to form helium

Shell of helium fusing to form carbon

Shell of carbon fusing to form oxygen

Shell of oxygen fusing to form silicon

Shell of silicon fusing to form iron core

Surface temperature about 3,000°C

Cooling, expanding outer layers glow red

Core of mainly iron at a temperature of 3–5 billion °C

LIFE OF A MASSIVE STAR OF ABOUT 10 SOLAR MASSES

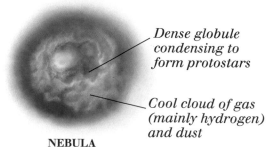

Dense globule condensing to form protostars

Cool cloud of gas (mainly hydrogen) and dust

NEBULA

Glowing ball of gas (mainly hydrogen)

Natal cocoon (shell of dust blown away by radiation from protostar)

PROTOSTAR
Duration: a few hundred thousand years

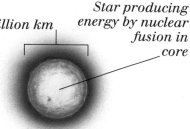

About 3 million km

Star producing energy by nuclear fusion in core

MAIN SEQUENCE STAR
Duration: 10 million years

FEATURES OF A SUPERNOVA

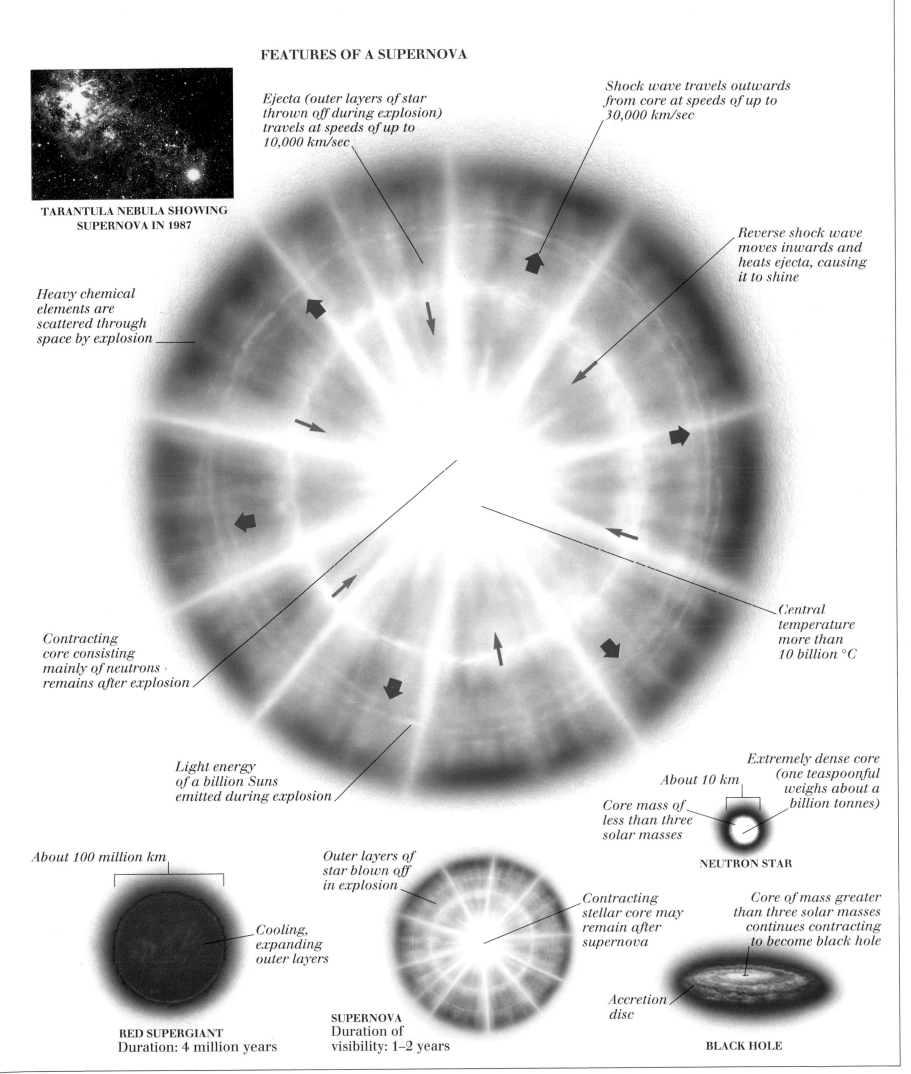

TARANTULA NEBULA SHOWING SUPERNOVA IN 1987

Ejecta (outer layers of star thrown off during explosion) travels at speeds of up to 10,000 km/sec

Shock wave travels outwards from core at speeds of up to 30,000 km/sec

Reverse shock wave moves inwards and heats ejecta, causing it to shine

Heavy chemical elements are scattered through space by explosion

Contracting core consisting mainly of neutrons remains after explosion

Central temperature more than 10 billion °C

Light energy of a billion Suns emitted during explosion

Extremely dense core (one teaspoonful weighs about a billion tonnes)

About 10 km

Core mass of less than three solar masses

NEUTRON STAR

About 100 million km

Outer layers of star blown off in explosion

Contracting stellar core may remain after supernova

Core of mass greater than three solar masses continues contracting to become black hole

Cooling, expanding outer layers

Accretion disc

RED SUPERGIANT
Duration: 4 million years

SUPERNOVA
Duration of visibility: 1–2 years

BLACK HOLE

23

Neutron stars and black holes

NEUTRON STARS AND BLACK HOLES form from the stellar cores that remain after stars have exploded as supernovae (see pp. 22-23). If the remaining core is between about one and a half and three solar masses, it contracts to form a neutron star. If the remaining core is greater than about three solar masses, it contracts to form a black hole. Neutron stars are typically only about 10 kilometres in diameter and consist almost entirely of subatomic particles called neutrons. Such stars are so dense that a teaspoonful would weigh about a billion tonnes. Neutron stars are observed as pulsars, so-called because they rotate rapidly and emit two beams of radio waves, which sweep across the sky and are detected as short pulses. Black holes are characterized by their extremely strong gravity, which is so powerful that not even light can escape; as a result, black holes are invisible. However, they may be detected if they have a close companion star. The gravity of the black hole pulls gas from the other star, forming an accretion disc that spirals around the black hole at high speed, heating up and emitting radiation. Eventually, the matter spirals in to cross the event horizon (the boundary of the black hole), thereby disappearing from the visible Universe.

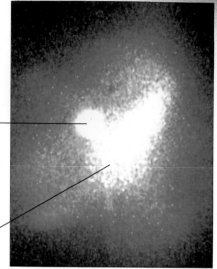

X-ray emission from pulsar (neutron star rotating 30 times each second)

X-ray emission from centre of nebula

X-RAY IMAGE OF THE CRAB NEBULA (SUPERNOVA REMNANT)

PULSAR (ROTATING NEUTRON STAR)

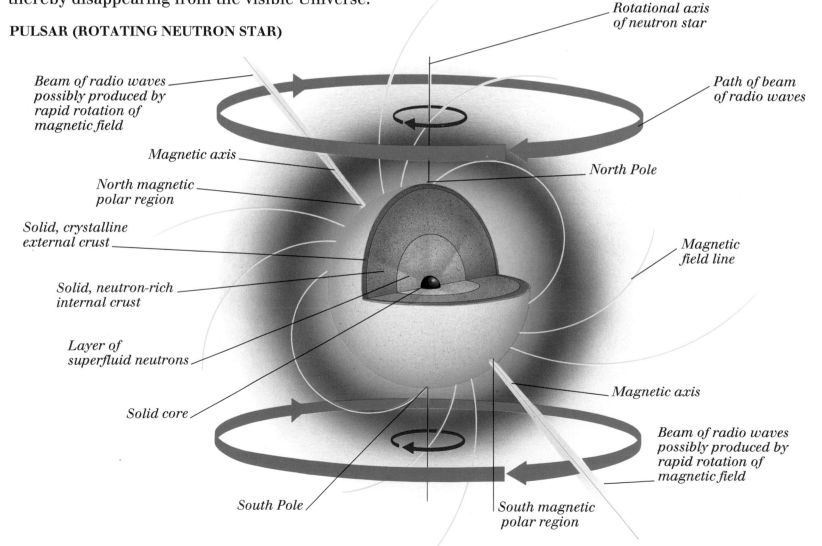

Rotational axis of neutron star

Beam of radio waves possibly produced by rapid rotation of magnetic field

Path of beam of radio waves

Magnetic axis

North Pole

North magnetic polar region

Solid, crystalline external crust

Magnetic field line

Solid, neutron-rich internal crust

Layer of superfluid neutrons

Magnetic axis

Solid core

Beam of radio waves possibly produced by rapid rotation of magnetic field

South Pole

South magnetic polar region

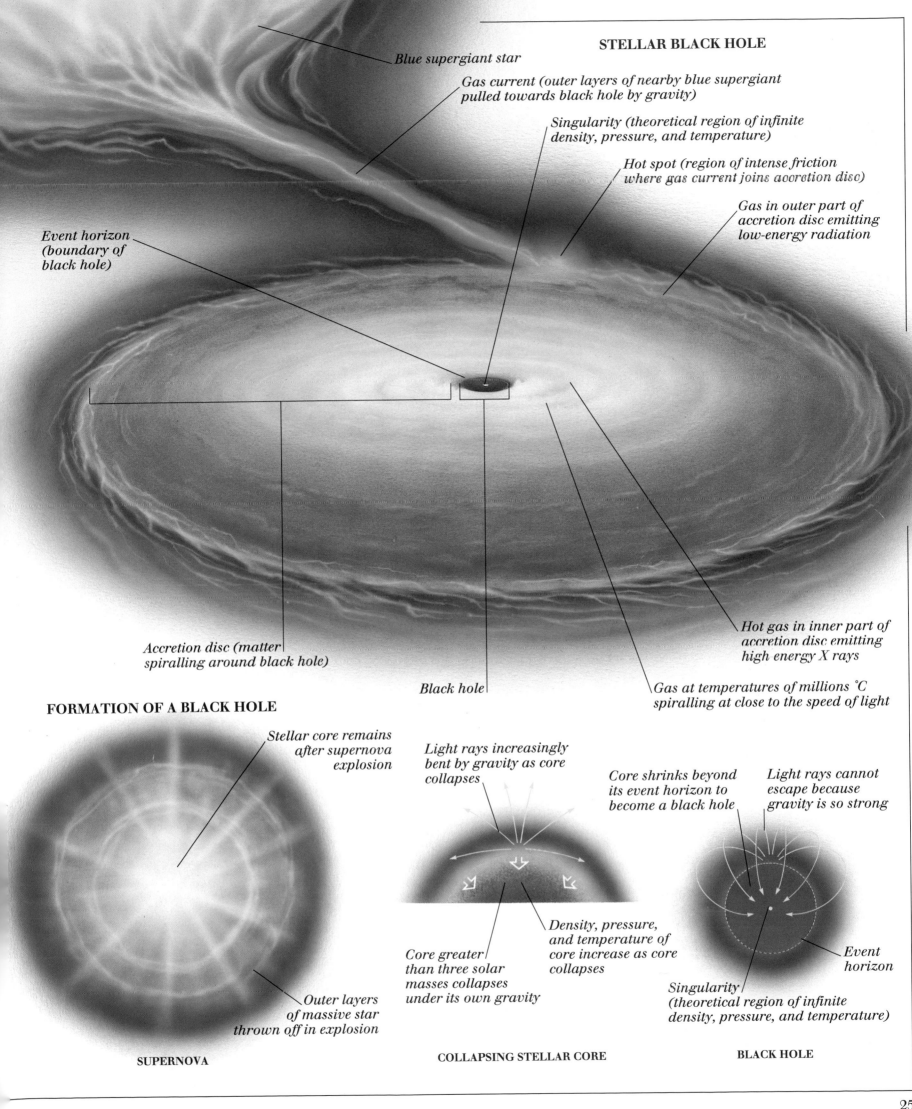

STELLAR BLACK HOLE

Blue supergiant star

Gas current (outer layers of nearby blue supergiant pulled towards black hole by gravity)

Singularity (theoretical region of infinite density, pressure, and temperature)

Hot spot (region of intense friction where gas current joins accretion disc)

Gas in outer part of accretion disc emitting low-energy radiation

Event horizon (boundary of black hole)

Accretion disc (matter spiralling around black hole)

Black hole

Hot gas in inner part of accretion disc emitting high energy X rays

Gas at temperatures of millions °C spiralling at close to the speed of light

FORMATION OF A BLACK HOLE

Stellar core remains after supernova explosion

Light rays increasingly bent by gravity as core collapses

Core shrinks beyond its event horizon to become a black hole

Light rays cannot escape because gravity is so strong

Density, pressure, and temperature of core increase as core collapses

Core greater than three solar masses collapses under its own gravity

Event horizon

Singularity (theoretical region of infinite density, pressure, and temperature)

Outer layers of massive star thrown off in explosion

SUPERNOVA

COLLAPSING STELLAR CORE

BLACK HOLE

25

The Solar System

THE SOLAR SYSTEM consists of a central star (the Sun) and the bodies that orbit it. These bodies include nine planets and their 61 known moons; asteroids; comets; and meteoroids. The Solar System also contains interplanetary gas and dust. Most of the planets fall into two groups: four small rocky planets near the Sun (Mercury, Venus, Earth, and Mars); and four planets further out, the gas giants (Jupiter, Saturn, Uranus, and Neptune). Pluto belongs to neither group but is very small, solid, and icy. Pluto is the outermost planet, except when it passes briefly inside Neptune's orbit. Between the rocky planets and gas giants is the asteroid belt, which contains thousands of chunks of rock orbiting the Sun. Most of the bodies in the Solar System move around the Sun in elliptical orbits located in a thin disc around the Sun's equator. All the planets orbit the Sun in the same direction (anticlockwise when viewed from above) and all but Venus, Uranus, and Pluto also spin about their axes in this direction. Moons also spin as they, in turn, orbit their planets. The entire Solar System orbits the centre of our galaxy, the Milky Way (see pp. 10-11).

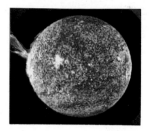

THE SUN

(see pp. 10-11)

PLANETARY ORBIT

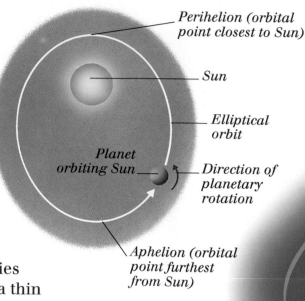

Perihelion (orbital point closest to Sun)

Sun

Elliptical orbit

Planet orbiting Sun

Direction of planetary rotation

Aphelion (orbital point furthest from Sun)

Aphelion of Neptune: 4,537 million km

ORBITS OF INNER PLANETS

Average orbital speed of Venus: 35.03 km/sec

Average orbital speed of Mercury: 47.89 km/sec

Average orbital speed of Earth: 29.79 km/sec

Average orbital speed of Mars: 24.13 km/sec

Mercury

Perihelion of Mercury: 45.9 million km

Perihelion of Venus: 107.4 million km

Perihelion of Earth: 147 million km

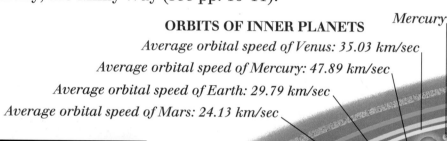

Mars

Perihelion of Mars: 206.7 million km

Earth

Venus

Sun

Aphelion of Mercury: 69.7 million km

Aphelion of Venus: 109 million km

Asteroid belt

Aphelion of Earth: 152 million km

Aphelion of Mars: 249 million km

Aphelion of Pluto: 7,375 million km

MERCURY
Year: 87.97 Earth days
Mass: 0.06 Earth masses
Diameter: 4,878 km

VENUS
Year: 224.7 Earth days
Mass: 0.81 Earth masses
Diameter: 12,103 km

EARTH
Year: 365.26 days
Mass: 1 Earth mass
Diameter: 12,756 km

MARS
Year: 1.88 Earth years
Mass: 0.11 Earth masses
Diameter: 6,786 km

JUPITER
Year: 11.86 Earth years
Mass: 317.94 Earth masses
Diameter: 142,984 km

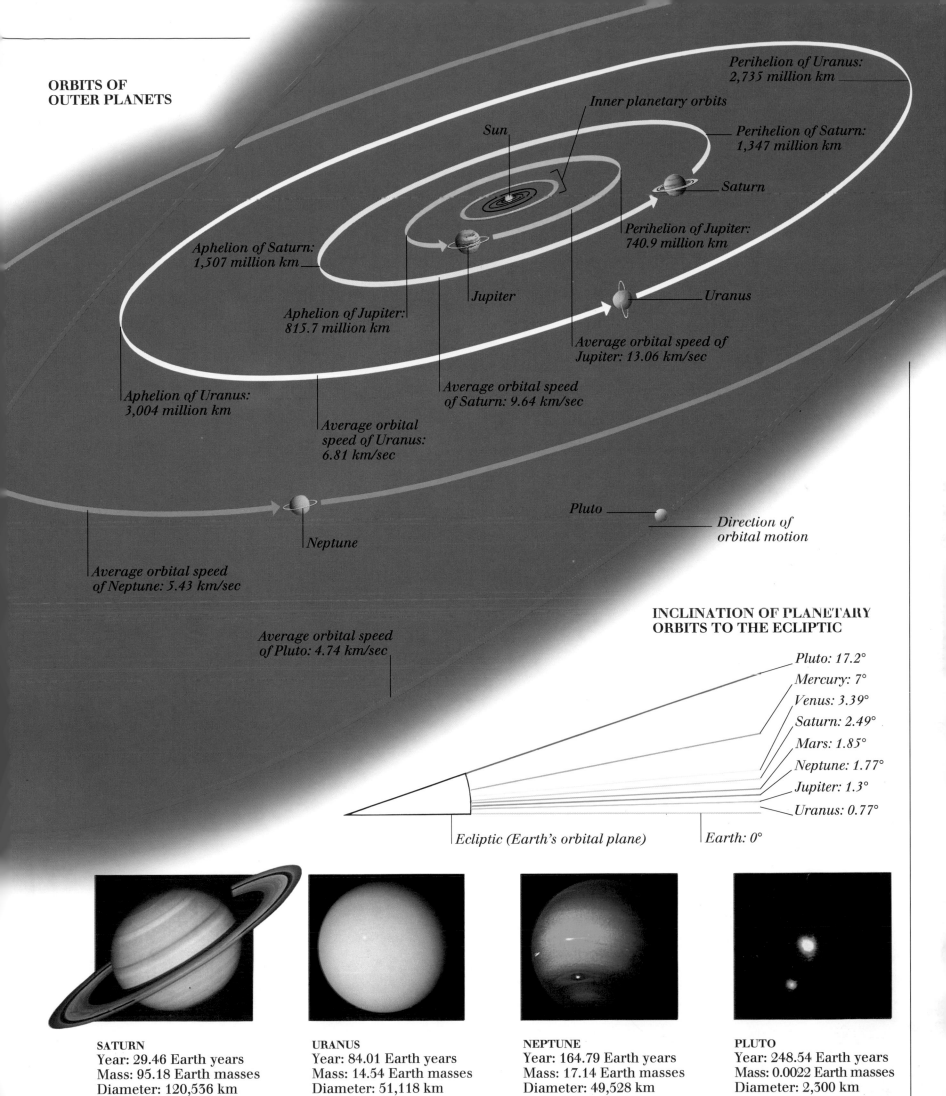

ORBITS OF OUTER PLANETS

Perihelion of Uranus: 2,735 million km

Inner planetary orbits

Sun

Perihelion of Saturn: 1,347 million km

Saturn

Perihelion of Jupiter: 740.9 million km

Jupiter

Aphelion of Saturn: 1,507 million km

Aphelion of Jupiter: 815.7 million km

Uranus

Aphelion of Uranus: 3,004 million km

Average orbital speed of Saturn: 9.64 km/sec

Average orbital speed of Jupiter: 13.06 km/sec

Average orbital speed of Uranus: 6.81 km/sec

Neptune

Pluto

Direction of orbital motion

Average orbital speed of Neptune: 5.43 km/sec

Average orbital speed of Pluto: 4.74 km/sec

INCLINATION OF PLANETARY ORBITS TO THE ECLIPTIC

Pluto: 17.2°
Mercury: 7°
Venus: 3.39°
Saturn: 2.49°
Mars: 1.85°
Neptune: 1.77°
Jupiter: 1.3°
Uranus: 0.77°

Ecliptic (Earth's orbital plane)

Earth: 0°

SATURN
Year: 29.46 Earth years
Mass: 95.18 Earth masses
Diameter: 120,536 km

URANUS
Year: 84.01 Earth years
Mass: 14.54 Earth masses
Diameter: 51,118 km

NEPTUNE
Year: 164.79 Earth years
Mass: 17.14 Earth masses
Diameter: 49,528 km

PLUTO
Year: 248.54 Earth years
Mass: 0.0022 Earth masses
Diameter: 2,300 km

The Sun

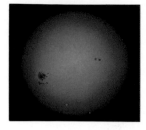

SOLAR PHOTOSPHERE

THE SUN IS THE STAR AT THE CENTRE of the Solar System. It is about five billion years old and will continue to shine as it does now for about another five billion years. The Sun is a yellow main sequence star (see pp. 18-19) about 1.4 million kilometres in diameter. It consists almost entirely of hydrogen and helium. In the Sun's core, hydrogen is converted to helium by nuclear fusion, releasing energy in the process. The energy travels from the core, through the radiative and convective zones, to the photosphere (visible surface), where it leaves the Sun in the form of heat and light. On the photosphere there are often dark, relatively cool areas called sunspots, which usually appear in pairs or groups and are thought to be caused by magnetic fields. Other types of solar activity are flares, which are usually associated with sunspots, and prominences. Flares are sudden discharges of high-energy radiation and atomic particles. Prominences are huge loops or filaments of gas extending into the solar atmosphere; some last for hours, others for months. Beyond the photosphere is the chromosphere (inner atmosphere) and the extremely rarified corona (outer atmosphere), which extends millions of kilometres into space. Tiny particles that escape from the corona give rise to the solar wind, which streams through space at hundreds of kilometres per second. The chromosphere and corona can be seen from Earth when the Sun is totally eclipsed by the Moon.

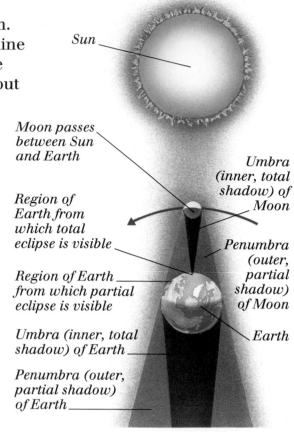

Sun

Moon passes between Sun and Earth

Umbra (inner, total shadow) of Moon

Region of Earth from which total eclipse is visible

Penumbra (outer, partial shadow) of Moon

Region of Earth from which partial eclipse is visible

Umbra (inner, total shadow) of Earth

Earth

Penumbra (outer, partial shadow) of Earth

SURFACE FEATURES

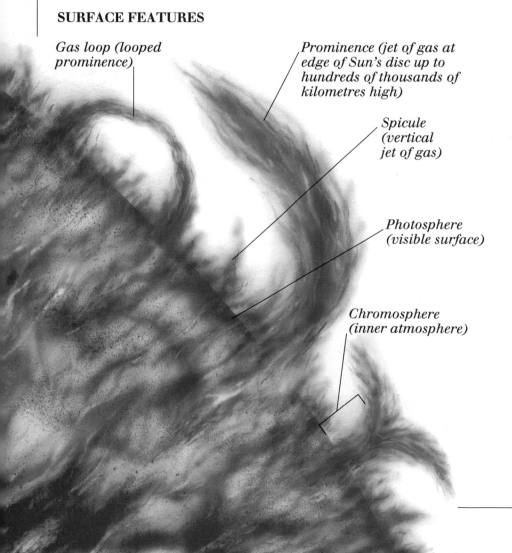

Gas loop (looped prominence)

Prominence (jet of gas at edge of Sun's disc up to hundreds of thousands of kilometres high)

Spicule (vertical jet of gas)

Photosphere (visible surface)

Chromosphere (inner atmosphere)

TOTAL SOLAR ECLIPSE

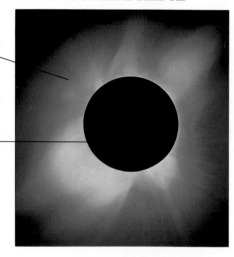

Corona (outer atmosphere of extremely hot, diffuse gas)

Moon covers Sun's disc

SUNSPOTS

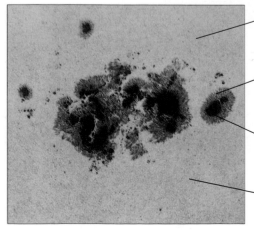

Granulated surface of Sun

Penumbra (lighter, outer region) containing radial fibrils

Umbra (darker, inner region) temperature about 4,000°C

Photosphere temperature about 5,500°C

EXTERNAL FEATURES AND INTERNAL STRUCTURE OF THE SUN

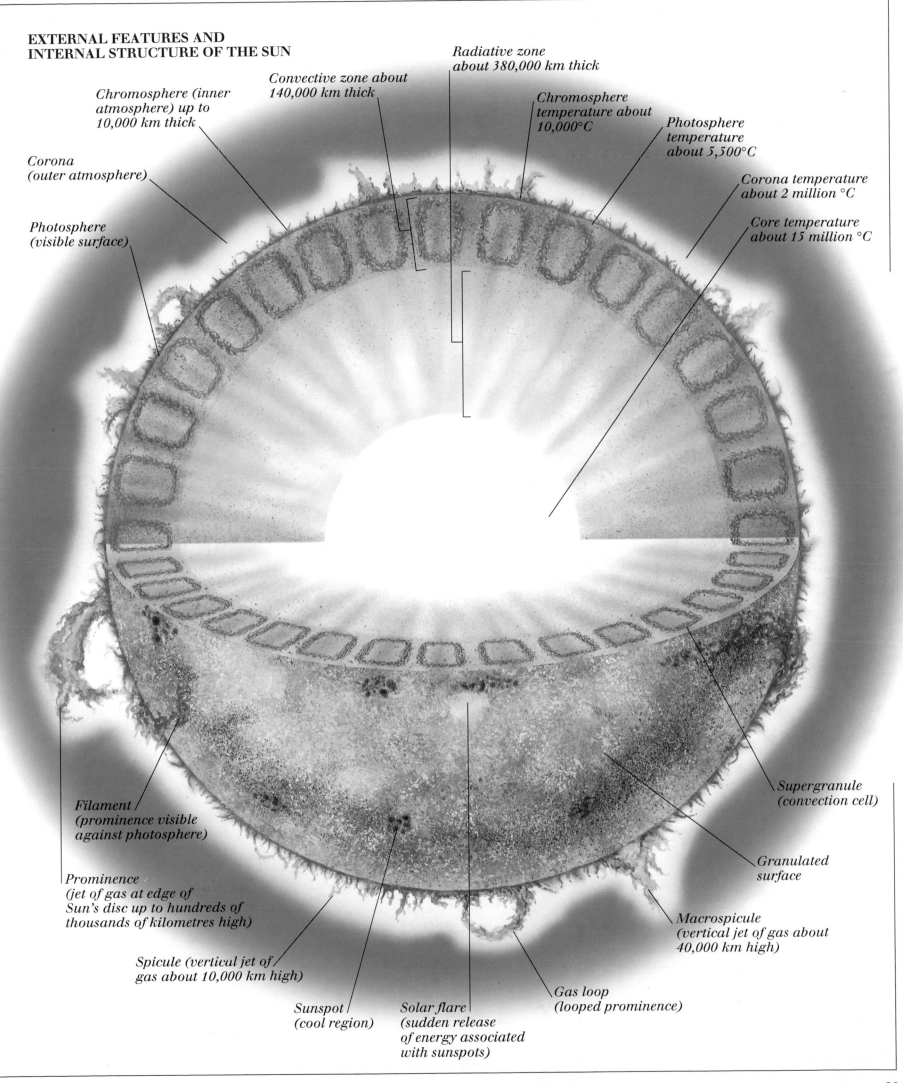

Chromosphere (inner atmosphere) up to 10,000 km thick

Convective zone about 140,000 km thick

Radiative zone about 380,000 km thick

Chromosphere temperature about 10,000°C

Photosphere temperature about 5,500°C

Corona (outer atmosphere)

Corona temperature about 2 million °C

Core temperature about 15 million °C

Photosphere (visible surface)

Supergranule (convection cell)

Filament (prominence visible against photosphere)

Granulated surface

Prominence (jet of gas at edge of Sun's disc up to hundreds of thousands of kilometres high)

Macrospicule (vertical jet of gas about 40,000 km high)

Spicule (vertical jet of gas about 10,000 km high)

Sunspot (cool region)

Solar flare (sudden release of energy associated with sunspots)

Gas loop (looped prominence)

Mercury

MERCURY

MERCURY IS THE NEAREST PLANET to the Sun, orbiting at an average distance of about 58 million kilometres. Because Mercury is the closest planet to the Sun, it moves faster than any other planet, travelling at an average speed of nearly 48 kilometres per second and completing an orbit in just under 88 days. Mercury is very small (only Pluto is smaller) and rocky. Most of the surface has been heavily cratered by the impact of meteorites, although there are also smooth, sparsely cratered plains. The Caloris Basin is the largest crater, measuring about 1,300 kilometres across. It is thought to have been formed when a rock the size of an asteroid hit the planet, and is surrounded by concentric rings of mountains thrown up by the impact. The surface also has many ridges (called rupes) that are thought to have been formed when the hot core of the young planet cooled and shrank about four billion years ago, buckling the planet's surface in the process. The planet rotates about its axis very slowly, taking nearly 59 Earth days to complete one rotation. As a result, a solar day (sunrise to sunrise) on Mercury is about 176 Earth days – twice as long as the 88-day Mercurian year. Mercury has extreme surface temperatures, ranging from a maximum of 430°C on the sunlit side to -170°C on the dark side. At nightfall, the temperature drops very quickly because the planet's atmosphere is almost non-existent. It consists only of minute amounts of helium and hydrogen captured from the solar wind, plus traces of other gases.

TILT AND ROTATION OF MERCURY

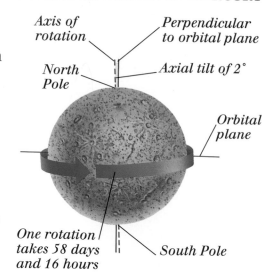

Axis of rotation

Perpendicular to orbital plane

North Pole

Axial tilt of 2°

Orbital plane

One rotation takes 58 days and 16 hours

South Pole

DEGAS AND BRONTË (RAY CRATERS)

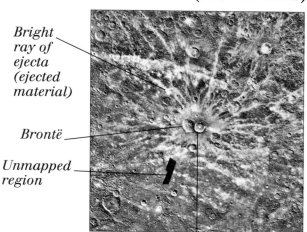

Bright ray of ejecta (ejected material)

Brontë

Unmapped region

Degas with central peak

FORMATION OF A RAY CRATER

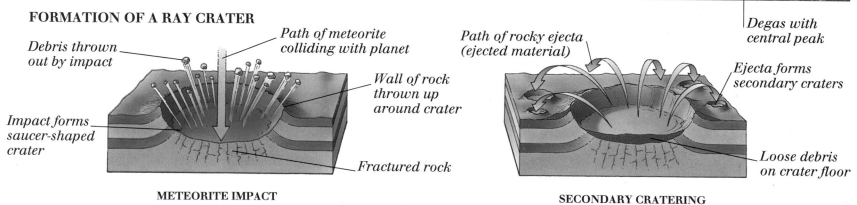

Debris thrown out by impact

Path of meteorite colliding with planet

Wall of rock thrown up around crater

Impact forms saucer-shaped crater

Fractured rock

METEORITE IMPACT

Path of rocky ejecta (ejected material)

Ejecta forms secondary craters

Loose debris on crater floor

SECONDARY CRATERING

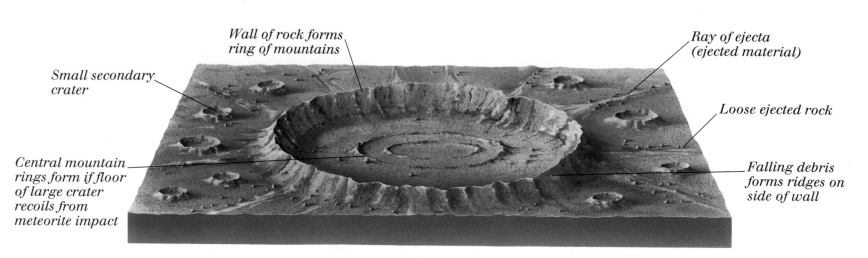

Wall of rock forms ring of mountains

Ray of ejecta (ejected material)

Small secondary crater

Loose ejected rock

Central mountain rings form if floor of large crater recoils from meteorite impact

Falling debris forms ridges on side of wall

RAY CRATER

COMPOSITION OF ATMOSPHERE

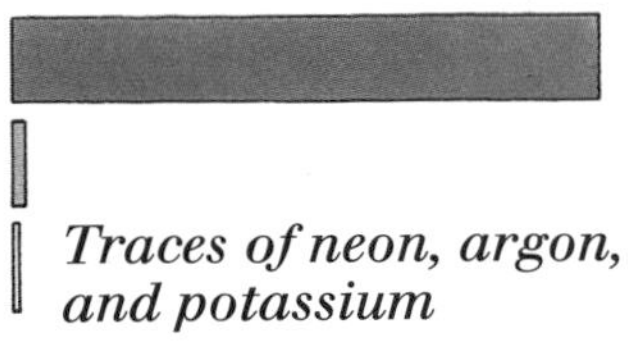

Principal constituents helium and hydrogen

Minor constituents sodium and oxygen

Traces of neon, argon, and potassium

CRATERS AND PLAINS NEAR MERCURY'S NORTH POLE

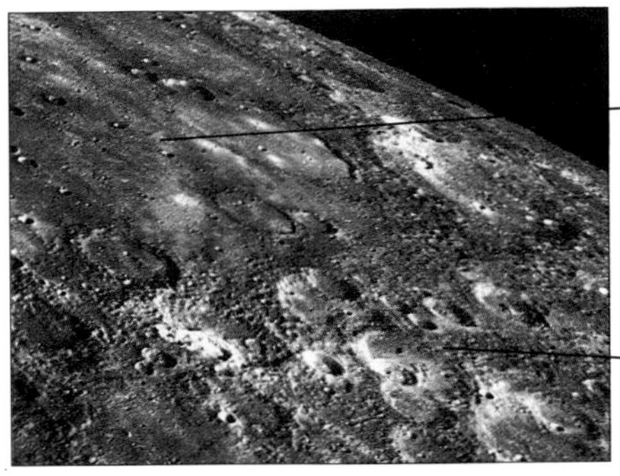

Borealis Planitia (smooth plain with a few young craters)

Terrain with many old craters

EXTERNAL FEATURES AND INTERNAL STRUCTURE OF MERCURY

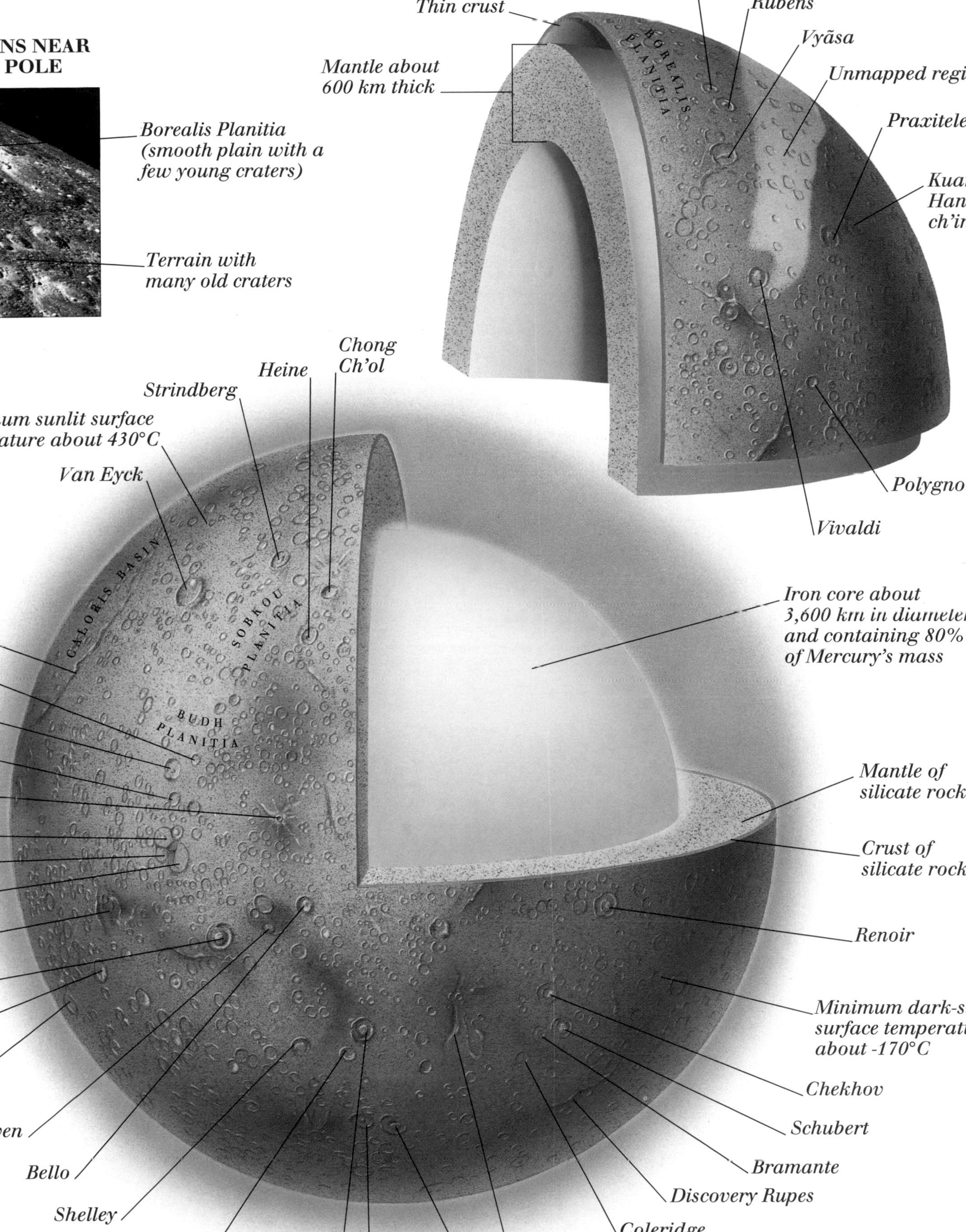

Thin crust

Mantle about 600 km thick

Monteverdi

Rubens

Vyāsa

Unmapped region

Praxiteles

Kuan Han-ch'ing

BOREALIS PLANITIA

Polygnotus

Vivaldi

Maximum sunlit surface temperature about 430°C

Strindberg

Heine

Chong Ch'ol

Van Eyck

Caloris Montes

Balzac

Phidias

Tyagaraja

Philoxenus

Zeami

Goya

Sophocles

Tolstoj

Vālmiki

Milton

Liang K'ai

Beethoven

Bello

Shelley

Hawthorne

Michelangelo

Wagner

Bach

Coleridge

Fram Rupes

Discovery Rupes

Bramante

Schubert

Chekhov

Minimum dark-side surface temperature about -170°C

Renoir

Crust of silicate rock

Mantle of silicate rock

Iron core about 3,600 km in diameter and containing 80% of Mercury's mass

CALORIS BASIN

SOBKOU PLANITIA

BUDH PLANITIA

31

Venus

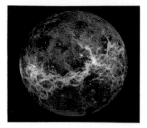

RADAR IMAGE OF VENUS

V ENUS IS A ROCKY PLANET and the second planet from the Sun. Venus spins slowly backwards as it orbits the Sun, causing its rotational period to be the longest in the Solar System, at about 243 Earth days. It is slightly smaller than Earth and probably has a similar internal structure, consisting of a semi-solid metal core, surrounded by a rocky mantle and crust. Venus is the brightest object in the sky after the Sun and Moon because its atmosphere reflects sunlight strongly. The main component of the atmosphere is carbon dioxide, which traps heat in a greenhouse effect far stronger than that on Earth. As a result, Venus is the hottest planet, with a maximum surface temperature of about 480°C. The thick cloud layers contain droplets of sulphuric acid and are driven around the planet by winds at speeds of up to 360 kilometres per hour. Although the planet takes 243 Earth days to rotate once, the high-speed winds cause the clouds to circle the planet in only four Earth days. The high temperature, acidic clouds, and enormous atmospheric pressure (about 90 times greater at the surface than that on Earth) make the environment extremely hostile. However, space probes have managed to land on Venus and photograph its dry, dusty surface. The Venusian surface has also been mapped by probes with radar equipment that can "see" through the cloud layers. Such radar maps reveal a terrain with craters, mountains, volcanoes, and areas where craters have been covered by plains of solidified volcanic lava. There are two large highland regions called Aphrodite Terra and Ishtar Terra.

TILT AND ROTATION OF VENUS

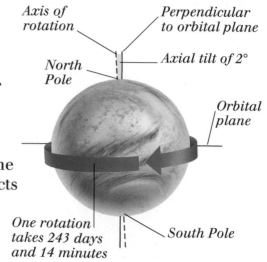

Axis of rotation

Perpendicular to orbital plane

North Pole

Axial tilt of 2°

Orbital plane

One rotation takes 243 days and 14 minutes

South Pole

CLOUD FEATURES

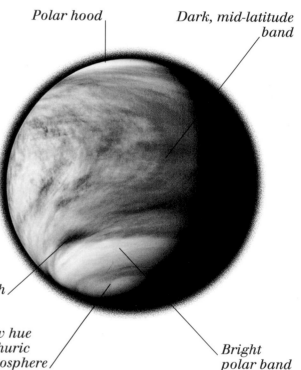

Polar hood

Dark, mid-latitude band

Cloud features swept around planet by winds of up to 360 km/h

Dirty yellow hue due to sulphuric acid in atmosphere

Bright polar band

VENUSIAN CRATERS

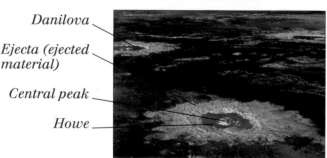

Danilova

Ejecta (ejected material)

Central peak

Howe

FALSE-COLOUR RADAR MAP OF THE SURFACE OF VENUS

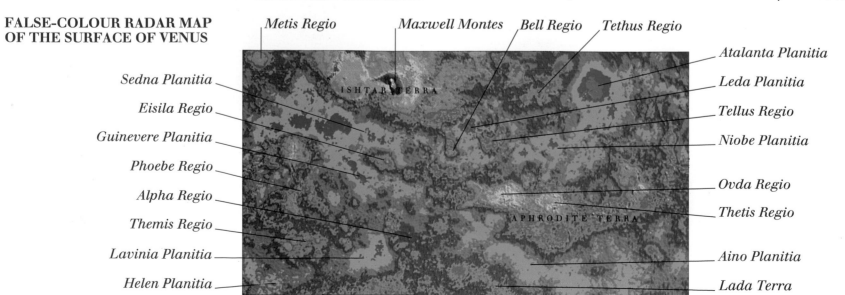

Metis Regio

Maxwell Montes

Bell Regio

Tethus Regio

Sedna Planitia

Atalanta Planitia

Eisila Regio

Leda Planitia

Guinevere Planitia

Tellus Regio

Phoebe Regio

Niobe Planitia

Alpha Regio

Themis Regio

Ovda Regio

Lavinia Planitia

Thetis Regio

Helen Planitia

Aino Planitia

Lada Terra

ISHTAR TERRA

APHRODITE TERRA

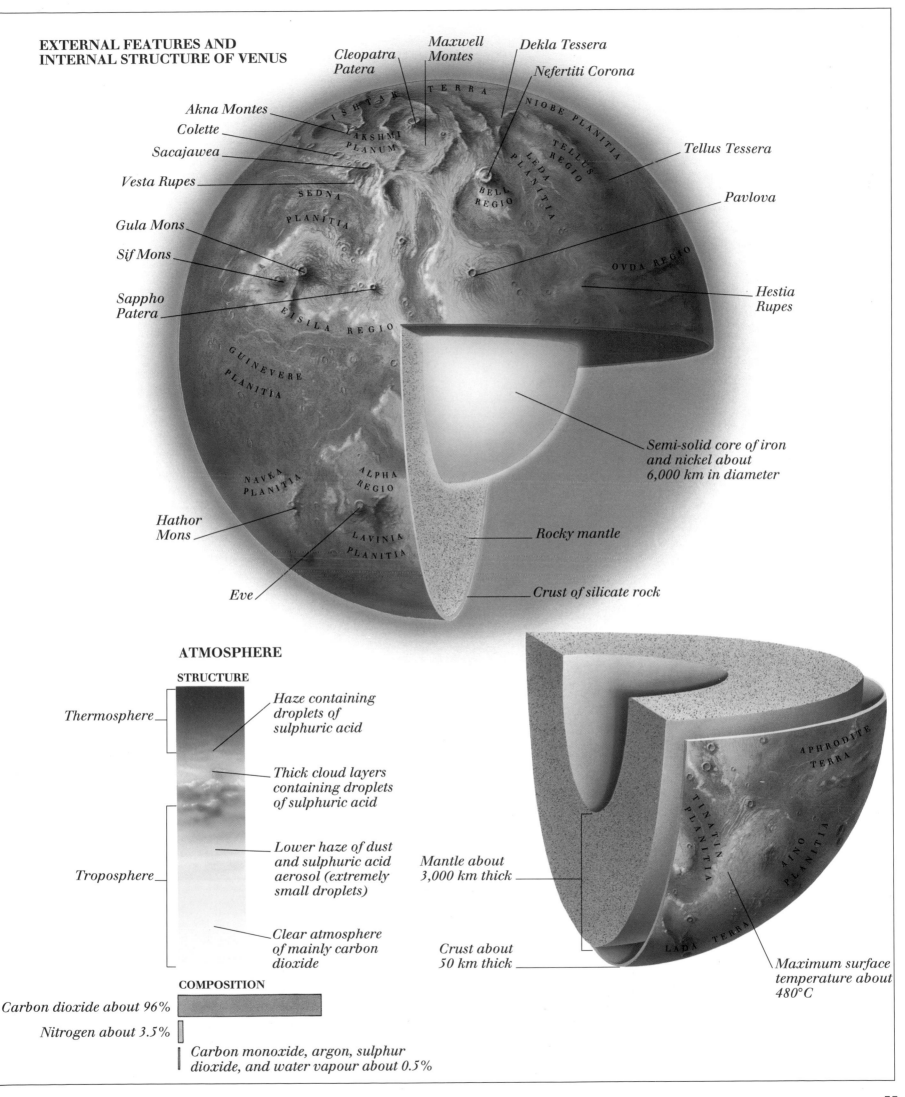

EXTERNAL FEATURES AND INTERNAL STRUCTURE OF VENUS

Cleopatra Patera
Maxwell Montes
Dekla Tessera
Nefertiti Corona
Akna Montes
Colette
Sacajawea
Vesta Rupes
Gula Mons
Sif Mons
Sappho Patera
Hathor Mons
Eve

ISHTAR TERRA
LAKSHMI PLANUM
NIOBE PLANITIA
TELLUS REGIO
LEDA PLANITIA
BELL REGIO
SEDNA PLANITIA
GUINEVERE PLANITIA
EISILA REGIO
NAVKA PLANITIA
ALPHA REGIO
LAVINIA PLANITIA
OVDA REGIO

Tellus Tessera
Pavlova
Hestia Rupes

Semi-solid core of iron and nickel about 6,000 km in diameter

Rocky mantle

Crust of silicate rock

ATMOSPHERE

STRUCTURE

Thermosphere
Troposphere

Haze containing droplets of sulphuric acid

Thick cloud layers containing droplets of sulphuric acid

Lower haze of dust and sulphuric acid aerosol (extremely small droplets)

Clear atmosphere of mainly carbon dioxide

Mantle about 3,000 km thick

Crust about 50 km thick

APHRODITE TERRA
TINATIN PLANITIA
AINO PLANITIA
LADA TERRA

Maximum surface temperature about 480°C

COMPOSITION

Carbon dioxide about 96%

Nitrogen about 3.5%

Carbon monoxide, argon, sulphur dioxide, and water vapour about 0.5%

The Earth

EARTH

THE EARTH IS THE THIRD planet from the Sun, the largest and densest rocky planet, and the only planet known to support life. The Earth's interior of rock and metal is typical of a rocky planet, but its crust is unusual, consisting of separate plates that slowly move relative to each other. Earthquakes and volcanic activity occur along the boundaries where the plates collide. The Earth's atmosphere acts as a protective blanket by blocking out harmful radiation from the Sun and stopping meteorites from reaching the planet's surface, but trapping enough heat to prevent extremes of cold. About 70 per cent of the Earth's surface is covered by water, which is not found in liquid form on the surface of any other planet. The Earth has one natural satellite, the Moon, which is large enough for both bodies to be considered a double-planet system.

TILT AND ROTATION OF THE EARTH

Axial tilt of 23.4°

Axis of rotation

North Pole

Orbital plane

One rotation takes 23 hours and 56 minutes

Perpendicular to orbital plane

South Pole

SATELLITE VIEWS OF THE EARTH (ATMOSPHERE NOT SHOWN)

North polar ice-cap

Tundra

North America

Tropical rainforest

Amazon River

South America

Andes

Atlantic Ocean

Europe

Sahara

Tropical rainforest

Africa

Grassland and scrubland

Antarctica

Asia

Pacific Ocean

Himalayas

Tropical rainforest

Indian Ocean

Australia

Grassland and shrubland

Desert

Antarctica

TOPOGRAPHY OF THE EARTH'S CRUST

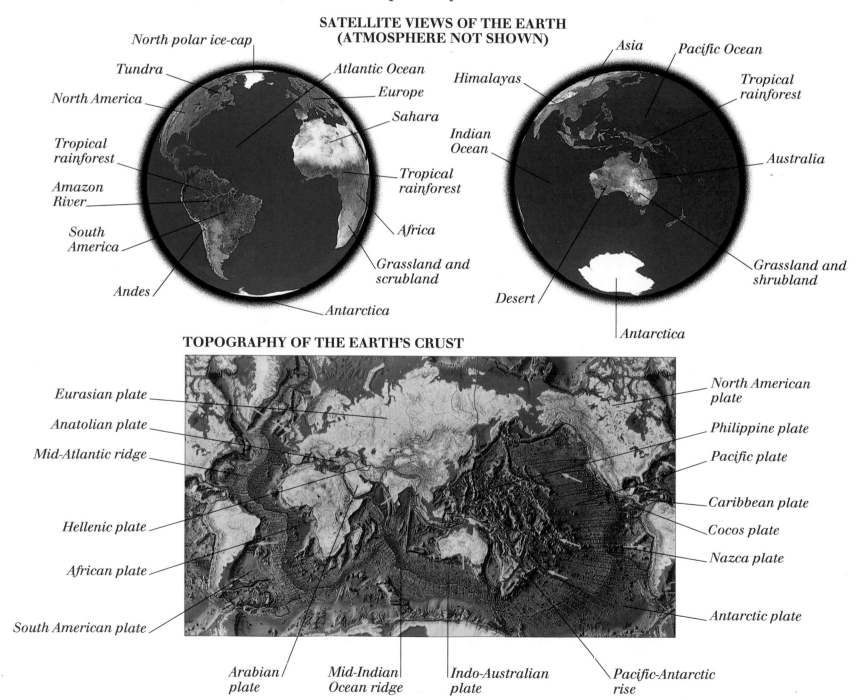

Eurasian plate

Anatolian plate

Mid-Atlantic ridge

Hellenic plate

African plate

South American plate

North American plate

Philippine plate

Pacific plate

Caribbean plate

Cocos plate

Nazca plate

Antarctic plate

Arabian plate

Mid-Indian Ocean ridge

Indo-Australian plate

Pacific-Antarctic rise

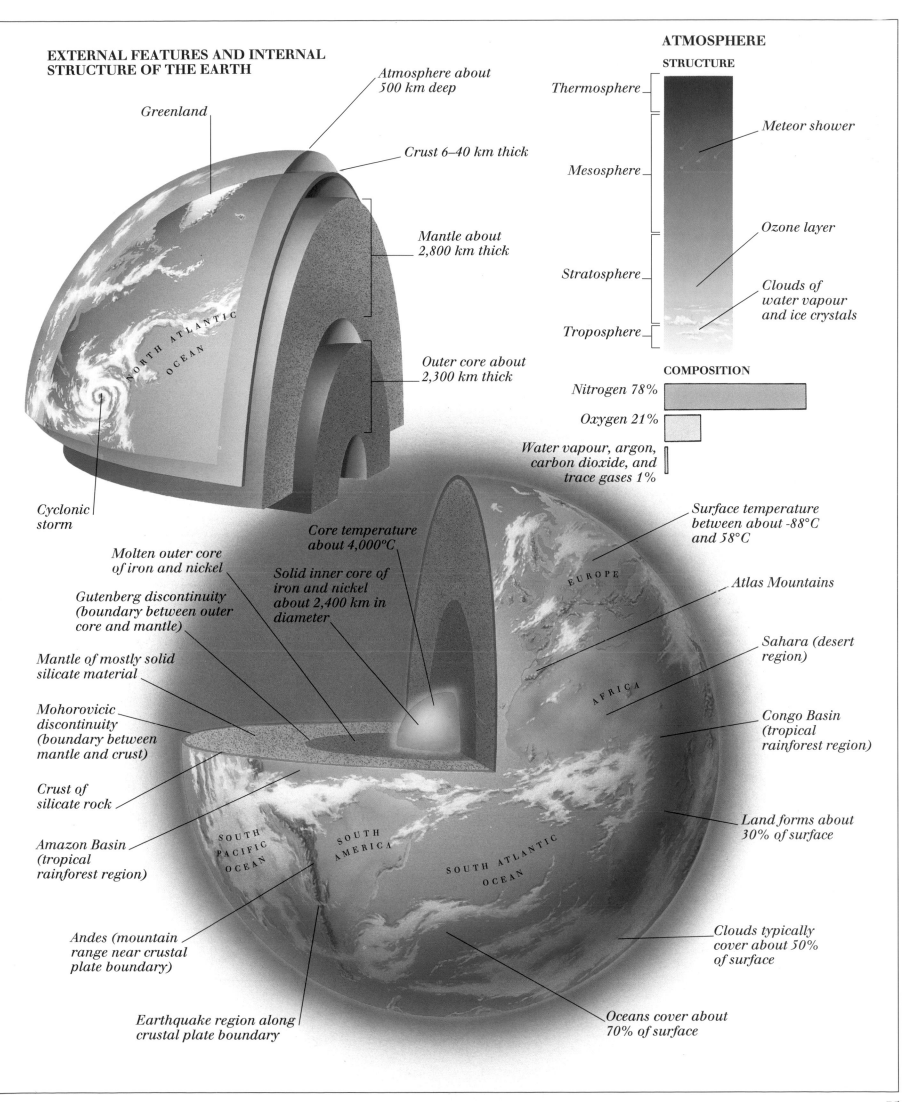

EXTERNAL FEATURES AND INTERNAL STRUCTURE OF THE EARTH

Greenland

Atmosphere about 500 km deep

Crust 6–40 km thick

Mantle about 2,800 km thick

Outer core about 2,300 km thick

NORTH ATLANTIC OCEAN

Cyclonic storm

Core temperature about 4,000°C

Molten outer core of iron and nickel

Solid inner core of iron and nickel about 2,400 km in diameter

Gutenberg discontinuity (boundary between outer core and mantle)

Mantle of mostly solid silicate material

Mohorovicic discontinuity (boundary between mantle and crust)

Crust of silicate rock

Amazon Basin (tropical rainforest region)

SOUTH PACIFIC OCEAN

SOUTH AMERICA

SOUTH ATLANTIC OCEAN

Andes (mountain range near crustal plate boundary)

Earthquake region along crustal plate boundary

ATMOSPHERE

STRUCTURE

Thermosphere

Mesosphere

Stratosphere

Troposphere

Meteor shower

Ozone layer

Clouds of water vapour and ice crystals

COMPOSITION

Nitrogen 78%

Oxygen 21%

Water vapour, argon, carbon dioxide, and trace gases 1%

Surface temperature between about -88°C and 58°C

EUROPE

Atlas Mountains

Sahara (desert region)

AFRICA

Congo Basin (tropical rainforest region)

Land forms about 30% of surface

Clouds typically cover about 50% of surface

Oceans cover about 70% of surface

The Moon

THE MOON FROM EARTH

THE MOON IS THE EARTH'S only natural satellite. It is relatively large for a moon, with a diameter of about 3,470 kilometres – just over a quarter that of the Earth. The Moon takes the same time to rotate on its axis as it takes to orbit the Earth (27.3 days), and so the same side (the near side) always faces us. However, the amount of the surface we can see – the phase of the Moon – depends on how much of the near side is in sunlight. The Moon is dry and barren, with no atmosphere or water. It consists mainly of solid rock, although its core may contain molten rock or iron. The surface is dusty, with highlands covered in craters caused by meteorite impacts, and lowlands in which large craters have been filled by solidified lava to form dark areas called maria or "seas". Maria occur mainly on the near side, which has a thinner crust than the far side. Many of the craters are rimmed by mountain ranges that form the crater walls and can be thousands of metres high.

TILT AND ROTATION OF THE MOON

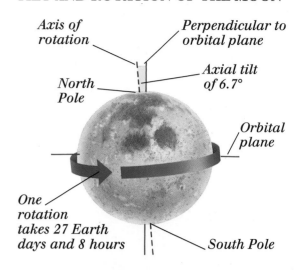

Axis of rotation
Perpendicular to orbital plane
North Pole
Axial tilt of 6.7°
Orbital plane
One rotation takes 27 Earth days and 8 hours
South Pole

CRATERS ON OCEANUS PROCELLARUM

Aristarchus
Cobra Head (head of Schröter's Valley)
Herodotus

NEAR SIDE OF THE MOON

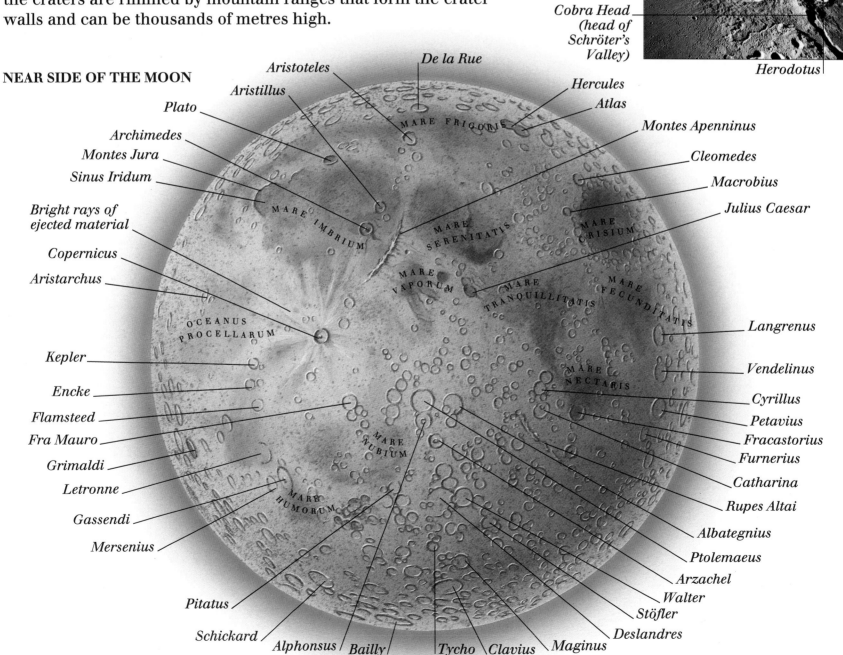

Aristoteles
De la Rue
Aristillus
Plato
Hercules
Atlas
Archimedes
Montes Apenninus
Montes Jura
Cleomedes
Sinus Iridum
Macrobius
Bright rays of ejected material
Julius Caesar
Copernicus
Aristarchus
MARE IMBRIUM
MARE SERENITATIS
MARE CRISIUM
MARE VAPORUM
MARE TRANQUILLITATIS
MARE FECUNDITATIS
OCEANUS PROCELLARUM
Langrenus
Kepler
Vendelinus
Encke
MARE NECTARIS
Flamsteed
Cyrillus
Fra Mauro
Petavius
Grimaldi
MARE NUBIUM
Fracastorius
Letronne
Furnerius
Gassendi
MARE HUMORUM
Catharina
Mersenius
Rupes Altai
Albategnius
Ptolemaeus
Arzachel
Walter
Pitatus
Stöfler
Schickard
Deslandres
Alphonsus
Bailly
Tycho
Clavius
Maginus

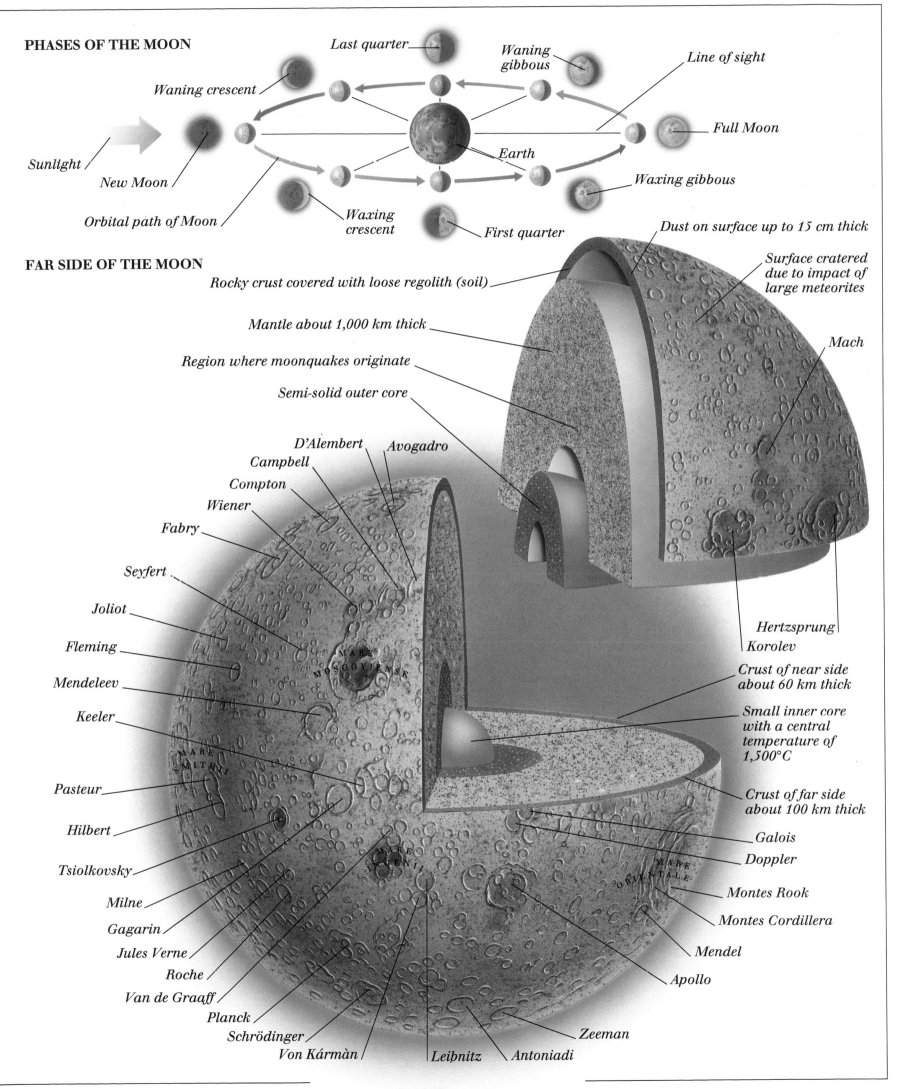

PHASES OF THE MOON

Last quarter

Waning gibbous

Line of sight

Waning crescent

Sunlight

Earth

Full Moon

New Moon

Waxing gibbous

Orbital path of Moon

Waxing crescent

First quarter

FAR SIDE OF THE MOON

Dust on surface up to 15 cm thick

Rocky crust covered with loose regolith (soil)

Surface cratered due to impact of large meteorites

Mantle about 1,000 km thick

Region where moonquakes originate

Mach

Semi-solid outer core

D'Alembert

Avogadro

Campbell

Compton

Wiener

Fabry

Seyfert

Joliot

Hertzsprung

Fleming

Korolev

Mendeleev

Crust of near side about 60 km thick

Keeler

MARE MOSCOVIENSE

Small inner core with a central temperature of 1,500°C

Pasteur

MARE SMYTHII

Crust of far side about 100 km thick

Hilbert

Galois

Tsiolkovsky

Doppler

Milne

MARE INGENII

MARE ORIENTALE

Gagarin

Montes Rook

Jules Verne

Montes Cordillera

Roche

Mendel

Van de Graaff

Apollo

Planck

Schrödinger

Zeeman

Von Kármàn

Leibnitz

Antoniadi

Mars

MARS

MARS, KNOWN AS THE RED PLANET, is the fourth planet from the Sun and the outermost rocky planet. In the 19th century, astronomers first observed what were thought to be signs of life on Mars. These signs included apparent canal-like markings on the surface, and dark patches that were thought to be vegetation. It is now known that the "canals" are an optical illusion, and the dark patches are areas where the red dust that covers most of the planet has been blown away. The fine dust particles are often whipped up by winds into dust storms that occasionally obscure almost all the surface. Residual dust in the atmosphere gives the Martian sky a pinkish hue. The northern hemisphere of Mars has many large plains formed of solidified volcanic lava, whereas the southern hemisphere has many craters and large impact basins. There are also several huge, extinct volcanoes, including Olympus Mons, which, at 600 kilometres across and 25 kilometres high, is the largest known volcano in the Solar System. The surface also has many canyons and branching channels. The canyons were formed by movements of the surface crust, but the channels are thought to have been formed by flowing water that has now dried up. The Martian atmosphere is much thinner than Earth's, with only a few clouds and morning mists. Mars has two tiny, irregularly shaped moons called Phobos and Deimos. Their small size indicates that they may be asteroids that have been captured by the gravity of Mars.

THE SURFACE OF MARS

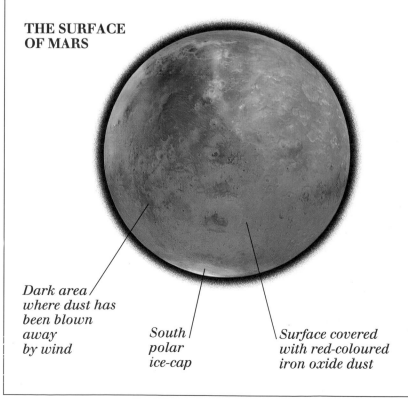

Dark area where dust has been blown away by wind

South polar ice-cap

Surface covered with red-coloured iron oxide dust

TILT AND ROTATION OF MARS

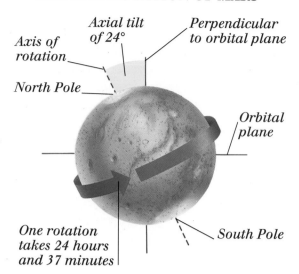

Axis of rotation

Axial tilt of 24°

Perpendicular to orbital plane

North Pole

Orbital plane

One rotation takes 24 hours and 37 minutes

South Pole

SURFACE FEATURES OF MARS

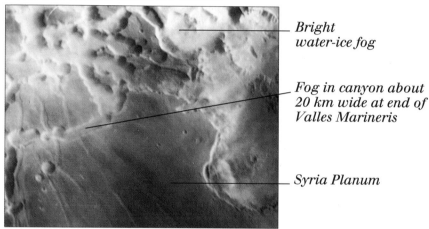

Bright water-ice fog

Fog in canyon about 20 km wide at end of Valles Marineris

Syria Planum

NOCTIS LABYRINTHUS (CANYON SYSTEM)

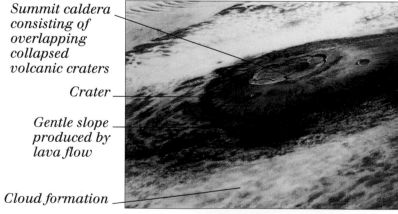

Summit caldera consisting of overlapping collapsed volcanic craters

Crater

Gentle slope produced by lava flow

Cloud formation

OLYMPUS MONS (EXTINCT SHIELD VOLCANO)

MOONS OF MARS

PHOBOS
Average diameter: 22 km
Average distance from planet: 9,400 km

DEIMOS
Average diameter: 13 km
Average distance from planet: 23,500 km

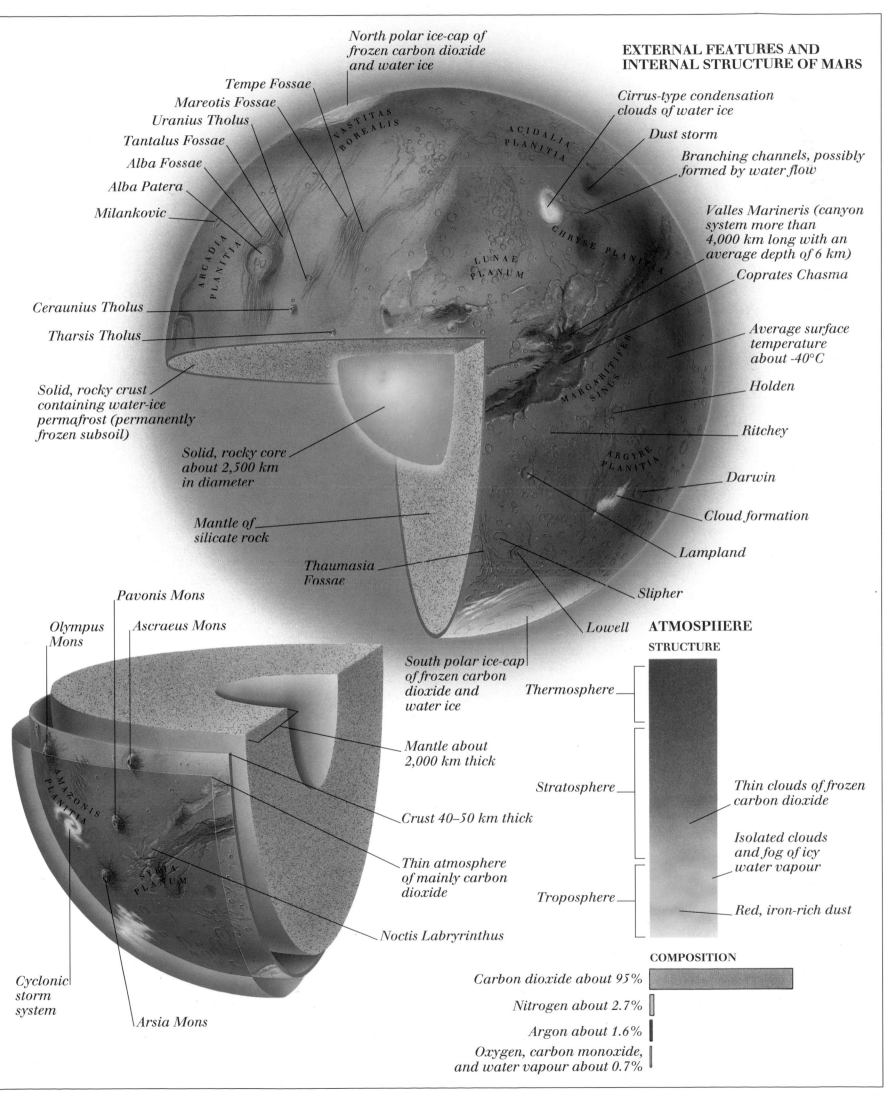

EXTERNAL FEATURES AND
INTERNAL STRUCTURE OF MARS

North polar ice-cap of
frozen carbon dioxide
and water ice

Tempe Fossae

Mareotis Fossae

Uranius Tholus

Tantalus Fossae

Alba Fossae

Alba Patera

Milankovic

Ceraunius Tholus

Tharsis Tholus

Solid, rocky crust
containing water-ice
permafrost (permanently
frozen subsoil)

Solid, rocky core
about 2,500 km
in diameter

Mantle of
silicate rock

Thaumasia
Fossae

VASTITAS BOREALIS

ACIDALIA PLANITIA

ARCADIA PLANITIA

LUNAE PLANUM

CHRYSE PLANITIA

MARGARITIFER SINUS

ARGYRE PLANITIA

Cirrus-type condensation
clouds of water ice

Dust storm

Branching channels, possibly
formed by water flow

Valles Marineris (canyon
system more than
4,000 km long with an
average depth of 6 km)

Coprates Chasma

Average surface
temperature
about -40°C

Holden

Ritchey

Darwin

Cloud formation

Lampland

Slipher

Lowell

South polar ice-cap
of frozen carbon
dioxide and
water ice

Mantle about
2,000 km thick

Crust 40–50 km thick

Thin atmosphere
of mainly carbon
dioxide

Noctis Labryrinthus

Olympus
Mons

Pavonis Mons

Ascraeus Mons

AMAZONIS PLANITIA

SYRIA PLANUM

Cyclonic
storm
system

Arsia Mons

ATMOSPHERE

STRUCTURE

Thermosphere

Stratosphere

Troposphere

Thin clouds of frozen
carbon dioxide

Isolated clouds
and fog of icy
water vapour

Red, iron-rich dust

COMPOSITION

Carbon dioxide about 95%

Nitrogen about 2.7%

Argon about 1.6%

Oxygen, carbon monoxide,
and water vapour about 0.7%

39

Jupiter

JUPITER

JUPITER IS THE FIFTH PLANET from the Sun and the first of the four gas giants. It is the largest and the most massive planet, with a diameter about 11 times that of the Earth and a mass about 2.5 times the combined mass of the eight other planets. Jupiter is thought to have a small rocky core surrounded by an inner mantle of metallic hydrogen (liquid hydrogen that acts like a metal). Outside the inner mantle is an outer mantle of liquid hydrogen and helium that merges into the gaseous atmosphere. Jupiter's rapid rate of rotation causes the clouds in its atmosphere to form belts and zones that encircle the planet parallel to the equator. Belts are dark, low-lying, relatively warm cloud layers, and zones are bright, high-altitude, cooler cloud layers. Within the belts and zones, turbulence causes the formation of cloud features such as white ovals and red spots, both of which are huge storm systems. The most prominent cloud feature is a storm called the Great Red Spot, which consists of a spiralling column of clouds three times wider than the Earth that rises about eight kilometres above the upper cloud layer. Jupiter has one thin, faint, main ring, inside which is a tenuous halo ring of tiny particles extending towards the planet. There are 16 known Jovian moons. The four largest moons (called the Galileans) are Ganymede, Callisto, Io, and Europa. Ganymede and Callisto are cratered and probably icy. Europa is smooth and icy and may contain water. Io is covered in bright red, orange, and yellow splotches. This colouring is caused by sulphurous material from active volcanoes that shoot plumes of lava hundreds of kilometres above the surface.

TILT AND ROTATION OF JUPITER

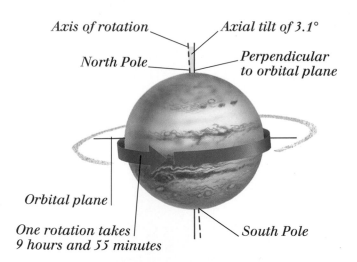

Axis of rotation

Axial tilt of 3.1°

North Pole

Perpendicular to orbital plane

Orbital plane

One rotation takes 9 hours and 55 minutes

South Pole

GREAT RED SPOT AND WHITE OVAL

Great Red Spot (anticyclonic storm system)

Red colour probably due to phosphorus

White oval (temporary anticyclonic storm system)

GALILEAN MOONS OF JUPITER

EUROPA
Diameter: 3,138 km
Average distance from planet: 670,900 km

CALLISTO
Diameter: 4,800 km
Average distance from planet: 1,880,000 km

GANYMEDE
Diameter: 5,262 km
Average distance from planet: 1,070,000 km

IO
Diameter: 3,642 km
Average distance from planet: 421,800 km

RINGS OF JUPITER

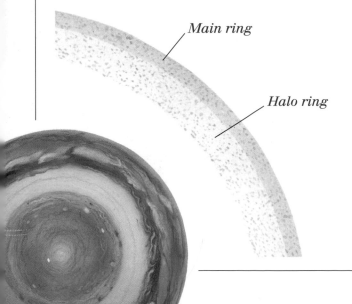

Main ring

Halo ring

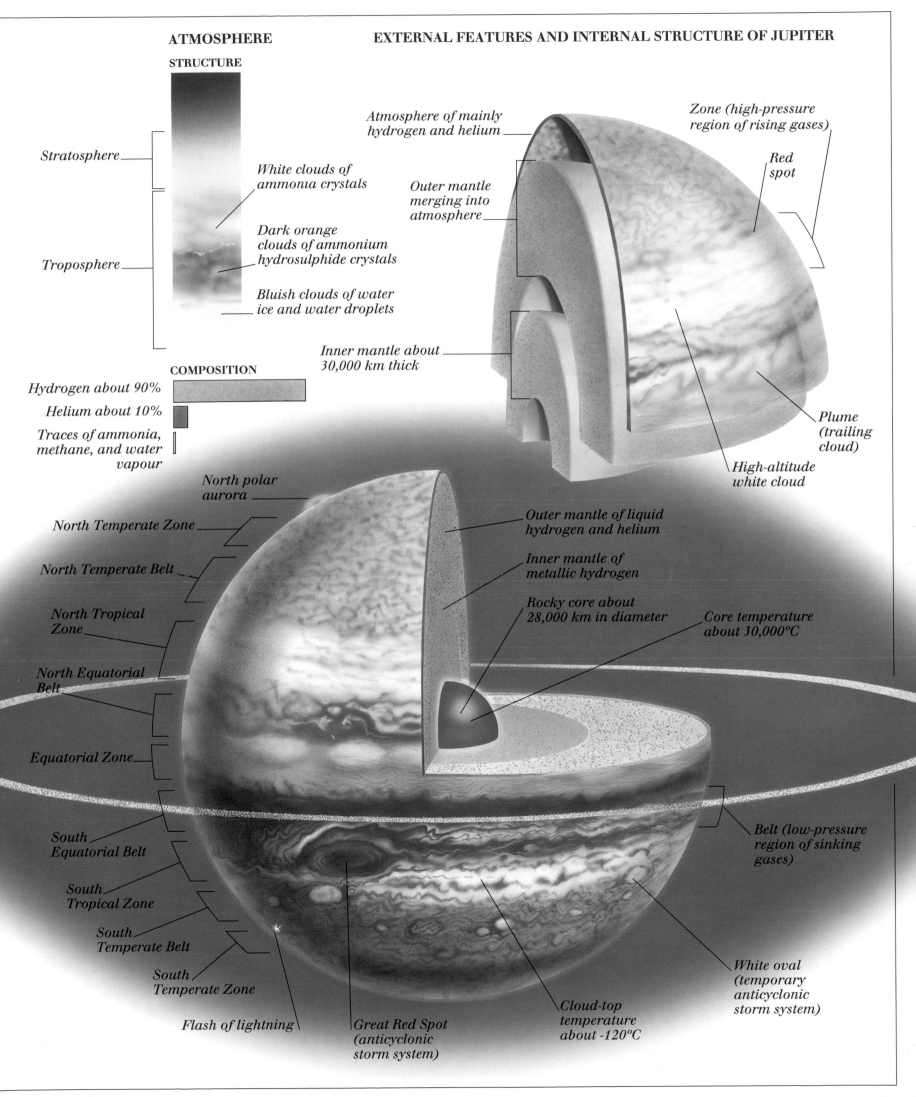

EXTERNAL FEATURES AND INTERNAL STRUCTURE OF JUPITER

ATMOSPHERE

STRUCTURE

Stratosphere

Troposphere

White clouds of ammonia crystals

Dark orange clouds of ammonium hydrosulphide crystals

Bluish clouds of water ice and water droplets

COMPOSITION

Hydrogen about 90%

Helium about 10%

Traces of ammonia, methane, and water vapour

Atmosphere of mainly hydrogen and helium

Outer mantle merging into atmosphere

Inner mantle about 30,000 km thick

Zone (high-pressure region of rising gases)

Red spot

Plume (trailing cloud)

High-altitude white cloud

North polar aurora

North Temperate Zone

North Temperate Belt

North Tropical Zone

North Equatorial Belt

Equatorial Zone

South Equatorial Belt

South Tropical Zone

South Temperate Belt

South Temperate Zone

Flash of lightning

Great Red Spot (anticyclonic storm system)

Outer mantle of liquid hydrogen and helium

Inner mantle of metallic hydrogen

Rocky core about 28,000 km in diameter

Core temperature about 30,000°C

Belt (low-pressure region of sinking gases)

White oval (temporary anticyclonic storm system)

Cloud-top temperature about -120°C

Saturn

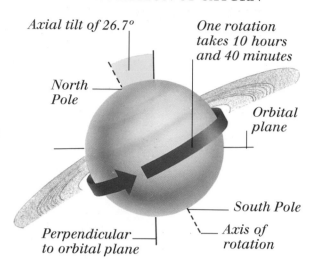

Axial tilt of 26.7°

One rotation takes 10 hours and 40 minutes

North Pole

Orbital plane

South Pole

Perpendicular to orbital plane

Axis of rotation

SATURN IS THE SIXTH PLANET from the Sun. It is a gas giant almost as big as Jupiter, with an equatorial diameter of about 120,500 kilometres. Saturn is thought to consist of a small core of rock and ice surrounded by an inner mantle of metallic hydrogen (liquid hydrogen that acts like a metal). Outside the inner mantle is an outer mantle of liquid hydrogen that merges into a gaseous atmosphere. Saturn's clouds form belts and zones similar to those on Jupiter, but obscured by overlying haze. Storms and eddies, seen as red or white ovals, occur in the clouds. Saturn has an extremely thin but wide system of rings that is less than one kilometre thick but extends outwards to about 420,000 kilometres from the planet's surface. The main rings comprise thousands of narrow ringlets, each made of icy lumps that range in size from tiny particles to chunks several metres across. The D, E, and G rings are very faint, the F ring is brighter, and the A, B, and C rings are bright enough to be seen from Earth with binoculars. Saturn has 18 known moons, some of which orbit inside the rings and are thought to exert a gravitational influence on the shapes of the rings. Unusually, seven of the moons are co-orbital – they share an orbit with another moon. Astronomers believe that such co-orbital moons may have originated from a single satellite that broke up.

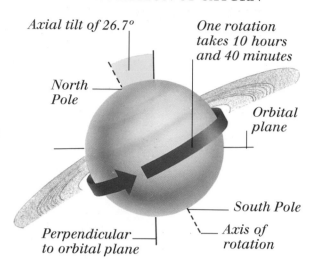

FALSE-COLOUR IMAGE OF SATURN

FALSE-COLOUR IMAGE OF SATURN'S CLOUD FEATURES

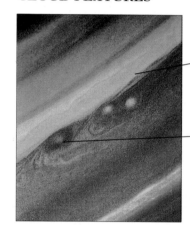

Ribbon-shaped striation caused by winds of up to 540 km/h

Oval (rotating storm system)

INNER RINGS OF SATURN

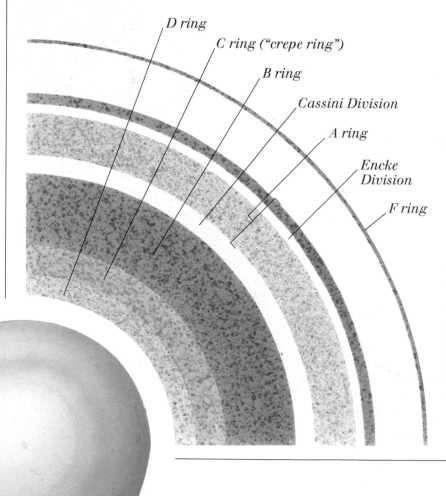

D ring

C ring ("crepe ring")

B ring

Cassini Division

A ring

Encke Division

F ring

MOONS OF SATURN

ENCELADUS
Diameter: 498 km
Average distance from planet: 238,000 km

TETHYS
Diameter: 1,050 km
Average distance from planet: 295,000 km

DIONE
Diameter: 1,118 km
Average distance from planet: 377,000 km

MIMAS
Diameter: 397 km
Average distance from planet: 186,000 km

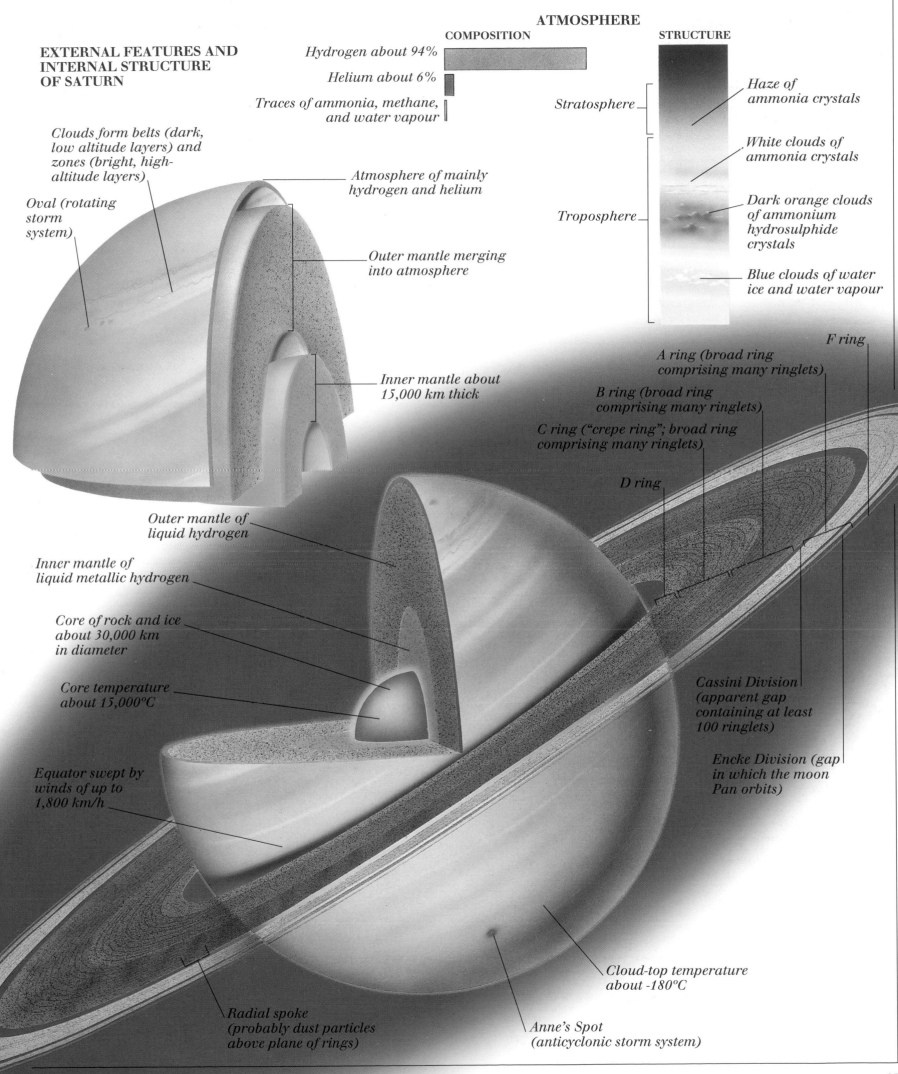

EXTERNAL FEATURES AND INTERNAL STRUCTURE OF SATURN

ATMOSPHERE

COMPOSITION

Hydrogen about 94%

Helium about 6%

Traces of ammonia, methane, and water vapour

STRUCTURE

Stratosphere

Troposphere

Haze of ammonia crystals

White clouds of ammonia crystals

Dark orange clouds of ammonium hydrosulphide crystals

Blue clouds of water ice and water vapour

Clouds form belts (dark, low altitude layers) and zones (bright, high-altitude layers)

Oval (rotating storm system)

Atmosphere of mainly hydrogen and helium

Outer mantle merging into atmosphere

Inner mantle about 15,000 km thick

F ring

A ring (broad ring comprising many ringlets)

B ring (broad ring comprising many ringlets)

C ring ("crepe ring"; broad ring comprising many ringlets)

D ring

Outer mantle of liquid hydrogen

Inner mantle of liquid metallic hydrogen

Core of rock and ice about 30,000 km in diameter

Core temperature about 15,000°C

Cassini Division (apparent gap containing at least 100 ringlets)

Encke Division (gap in which the moon Pan orbits)

Equator swept by winds of up to 1,800 km/h

Cloud-top temperature about -180°C

Radial spoke (probably dust particles above plane of rings)

Anne's Spot (anticyclonic storm system)

Uranus

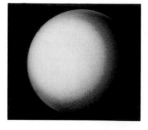

FALSE-COLOUR IMAGE OF URANUS

URANUS IS THE SEVENTH PLANET from the Sun and the third largest, with a diameter of about 51,000 kilometres. It is thought to consist of a dense mixture of different types of ice and gas around a solid core. Its atmosphere contains traces of methane, giving the planet a blue-green hue, and the temperature at the cloud tops is about -210°C. Uranus is the most featureless planet to have been closely observed: only a few icy clouds of methane have been seen so far. Uranus is unique among the planets in that its axis of rotation lies close to its orbital plane. As a result of its strongly tilted rotational axis, Uranus rolls on its side along its orbital path around the Sun, whereas other planets spin more or less upright. Uranus is encircled by 11 rings that consist of rocks interspersed with dust lanes. The rings contain some of the darkest matter in the Solar System and are extremely narrow, making them difficult to detect: nine of them are less than 10 kilometres wide, whereas most of Saturn's rings are thousands of kilometres in width. There are 15 known Uranian moons, all of which are icy and most of which are further out than the rings. The 10 inner moons are small and dark, with diameters of less than 160 kilometres, and the five outer moons are between about 470 and 1,600 kilometres in diameter. The outer moons have a wide variety of surface features. Miranda has the most varied surface, with cratered areas broken up by huge ridges and cliffs 20 kilometres high.

TILT AND ROTATION OF URANUS

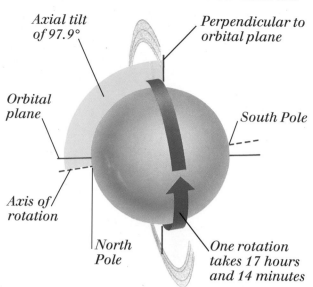

Axial tilt of 97.9°

Perpendicular to orbital plane

Orbital plane

South Pole

Axis of rotation

North Pole

One rotation takes 17 hours and 14 minutes

OUTER MOONS

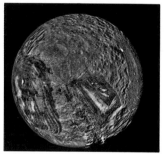

MIRANDA
Diameter: 472 km
Average distance from planet: 129,800 km

RINGS OF URANUS

Epsilon ring

Ring 1986 U1R

Delta ring

Gamma ring

Eta ring

Beta ring

Alpha ring

Rings 4 and 5

Ring 6

Ring 1986 U2R

RINGS AND DUST LANES

ARIEL
Diameter: 1,158 km
Average distance from planet: 191,200 km

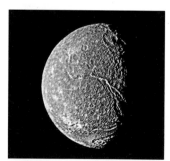

TITANIA
Diameter: 1,578 km
Average distance from planet: 435,900 km

UMBRIEL
Diameter: 1,169 km
Average distance from planet: 266,000 km

OBERON
Diameter: 1,523 km
Average distance from planet: 582,600 km

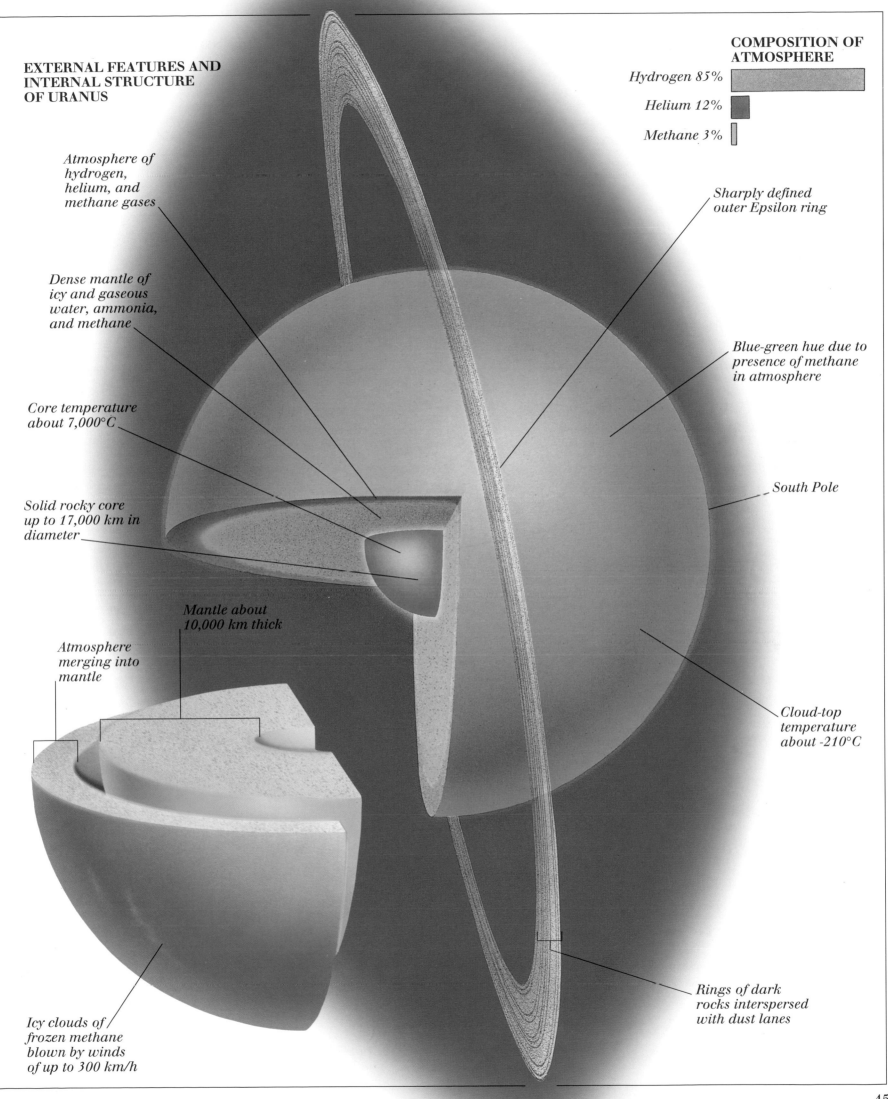

EXTERNAL FEATURES AND INTERNAL STRUCTURE OF URANUS

COMPOSITION OF ATMOSPHERE

Hydrogen 85%

Helium 12%

Methane 3%

Atmosphere of hydrogen, helium, and methane gases

Dense mantle of icy and gaseous water, ammonia, and methane

Core temperature about 7,000°C

Solid rocky core up to 17,000 km in diameter

Mantle about 10,000 km thick

Atmosphere merging into mantle

Icy clouds of frozen methane blown by winds of up to 300 km/h

Sharply defined outer Epsilon ring

Blue-green hue due to presence of methane in atmosphere

South Pole

Cloud-top temperature about -210°C

Rings of dark rocks interspersed with dust lanes

Neptune and Pluto

FALSE-COLOUR IMAGE OF NEPTUNE

NEPTUNE AND PLUTO are the two furthest planets from the Sun, at an average distance of about 4,500 million kilometres and 5,900 million kilometres respectively. Neptune is a gas giant and is thought to consist of a small rocky core surrounded by a mixture of liquids and gases. The atmosphere contains several prominent cloud features. The largest of these are the Great Dark Spot, which is as wide as the Earth, the Small Dark Spot, and the Scooter. The Great and Small Dark Spots are huge storms that are swept around the planet by winds of about 2,000 kilometres per hour. The Scooter is a large area of cirrus cloud. Neptune has four tenuous rings and eight known moons. Triton is the largest Neptunian moon and the coldest object in the Solar System, with a temperature of -235°C. Unlike most moons in the Solar System, Triton orbits its mother planet in the opposite direction to the planet's rotation. Pluto is usually the outermost planet but its elliptical orbit causes it to pass inside the orbit of Neptune for 20 years of its 248-year orbit. Pluto is so small and far away that little is known about it. It is a rocky planet, probably covered with ice and frozen methane. Pluto's only known moon, Charon, is large for a moon, at half the size of its parent planet. Because of the small difference in their sizes, Pluto and Charon are sometimes considered to be a double-planet system.

TILT AND ROTATION OF NEPTUNE

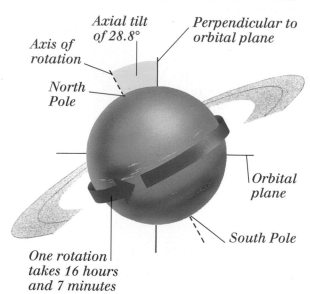

Axial tilt of 28.8°

Perpendicular to orbital plane

Axis of rotation

North Pole

Orbital plane

South Pole

One rotation takes 16 hours and 7 minutes

CLOUD FEATURES OF NEPTUNE

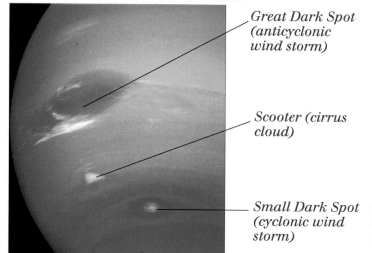

Great Dark Spot (anticyclonic wind storm)

Scooter (cirrus cloud)

Small Dark Spot (cyclonic wind storm)

HIGH-ALTITUDE CLOUDS

Methane cirrus clouds 40 km above main cloud deck

Cloud shadow

Main cloud deck blown by winds at speeds of about 2,000 km/h

RINGS OF NEPTUNE

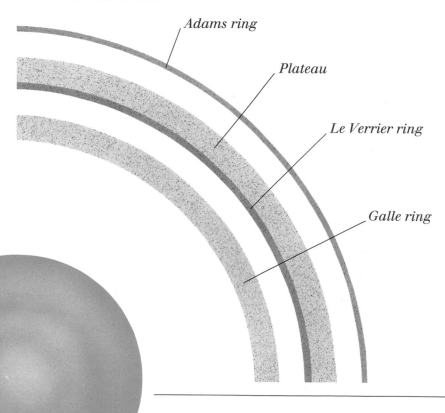

Adams ring

Plateau

Le Verrier ring

Galle ring

MOONS OF NEPTUNE

TRITON
Diameter: 2,705 km
Average distance from planet: 354,800 km

PROTEUS
Diameter: 416 km
Average distance from planet: 117,600 km

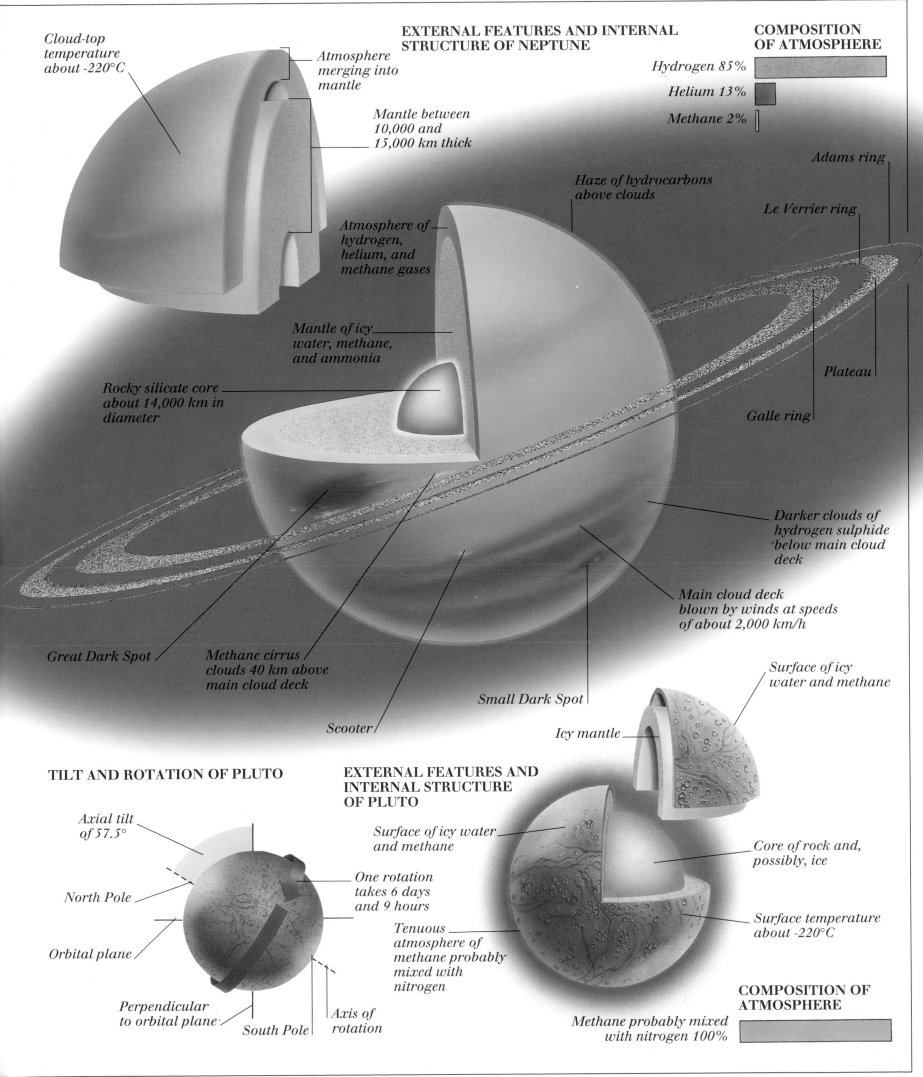

EXTERNAL FEATURES AND INTERNAL
STRUCTURE OF NEPTUNE

COMPOSITION
OF ATMOSPHERE

Hydrogen 85%

Helium 13%

Methane 2%

Cloud-top
temperature
about -220°C

Atmosphere merging into
mantle

Mantle between
10,000 and
15,000 km thick

Haze of hydrocarbons
above clouds

Adams ring

Le Verrier ring

Atmosphere of
hydrogen,
helium, and
methane gases

Mantle of icy
water, methane,
and ammonia

Plateau

Rocky silicate core
about 14,000 km in
diameter

Galle ring

Darker clouds of
hydrogen sulphide
below main cloud
deck

Main cloud deck
blown by winds at speeds
of about 2,000 km/h

Great Dark Spot

Methane cirrus
clouds 40 km above
main cloud deck

Small Dark Spot

Scooter

Surface of icy
water and methane

Icy mantle

TILT AND ROTATION OF PLUTO

EXTERNAL FEATURES AND
INTERNAL STRUCTURE
OF PLUTO

Axial tilt
of 57.5°

Surface of icy water
and methane

Core of rock and,
possibly, ice

North Pole

One rotation
takes 6 days
and 9 hours

Orbital plane

Surface temperature
about -220°C

Tenuous
atmosphere of
methane probably
mixed with
nitrogen

Perpendicular
to orbital plane

Axis of
rotation

South Pole

COMPOSITION OF
ATMOSPHERE

Methane probably mixed
with nitrogen 100%

Asteroids, comets, and meteoroids

ASTEROIDS, COMETS, AND METEOROIDS are all debris remaining from the nebula in which the Solar System formed 4.6 billion years ago. Asteroids are rocky bodies up to about 1,000 kilometres in diameter, although most are much smaller. Most of them orbit the Sun in the asteroid belt, which lies between the orbits of Mars and Jupiter. Comets may originate in a huge cloud (called the Oort Cloud) that is thought to surround the Solar System. They are made of frozen gases and dust, and are a few kilometres in diameter.

Occasionally, a comet is deflected from the Oort Cloud to orbit the Sun in a long, elliptical path. As the comet approaches the Sun, the comet's surface starts to vaporize in the heat, producing a brightly shining coma (a huge sphere of gas and dust around the nucleus), a gas tail, and a dust tail. Meteoroids are small chunks of stone or stone and iron, some of which are fragments of asteroids or comets. Meteoroids range in size from tiny dust particles to objects tens of metres across. If a meteoroid enters the Earth's atmosphere, it is heated by friction and appears as a glowing streak of light called a meteor (also known as a shooting star). Meteor showers occur when the Earth passes through the trail of dust particles left by a comet. Most meteors burn up in the atmosphere. The few that are large enough to reach the Earth's surface are termed meteorites.

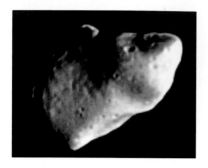

ASTEROID 951 GASPRA

OPTICAL IMAGE OF HALLEY'S COMET

FALSE-COLOUR IMAGE OF HALLEY'S COMET

High-intensity light emission

Nucleus

Medium-intensity light emission

Low-intensity light emission

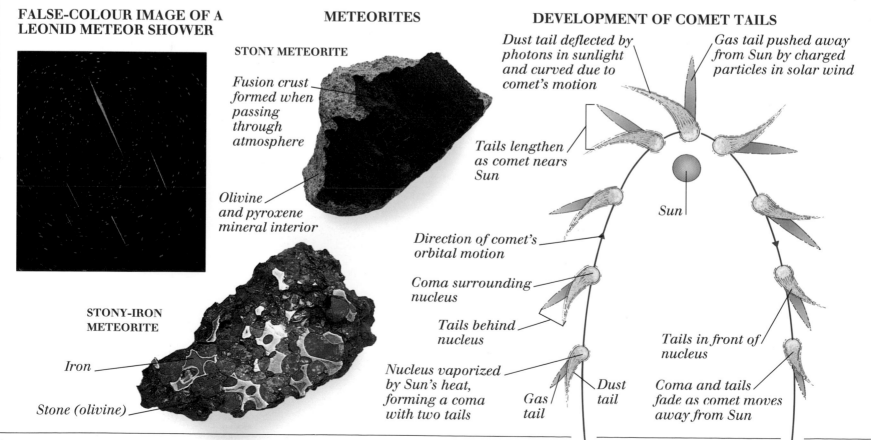

FALSE-COLOUR IMAGE OF A LEONID METEOR SHOWER

METEORITES

STONY METEORITE

Fusion crust formed when passing through atmosphere

Olivine and pyroxene mineral interior

STONY-IRON METEORITE

Iron

Stone (olivine)

DEVELOPMENT OF COMET TAILS

Dust tail deflected by photons in sunlight and curved due to comet's motion

Gas tail pushed away from Sun by charged particles in solar wind

Tails lengthen as comet nears Sun

Sun

Direction of comet's orbital motion

Coma surrounding nucleus

Tails behind nucleus

Tails in front of nucleus

Nucleus vaporized by Sun's heat, forming a coma with two tails

Gas tail

Dust tail

Coma and tails fade as comet moves away from Sun

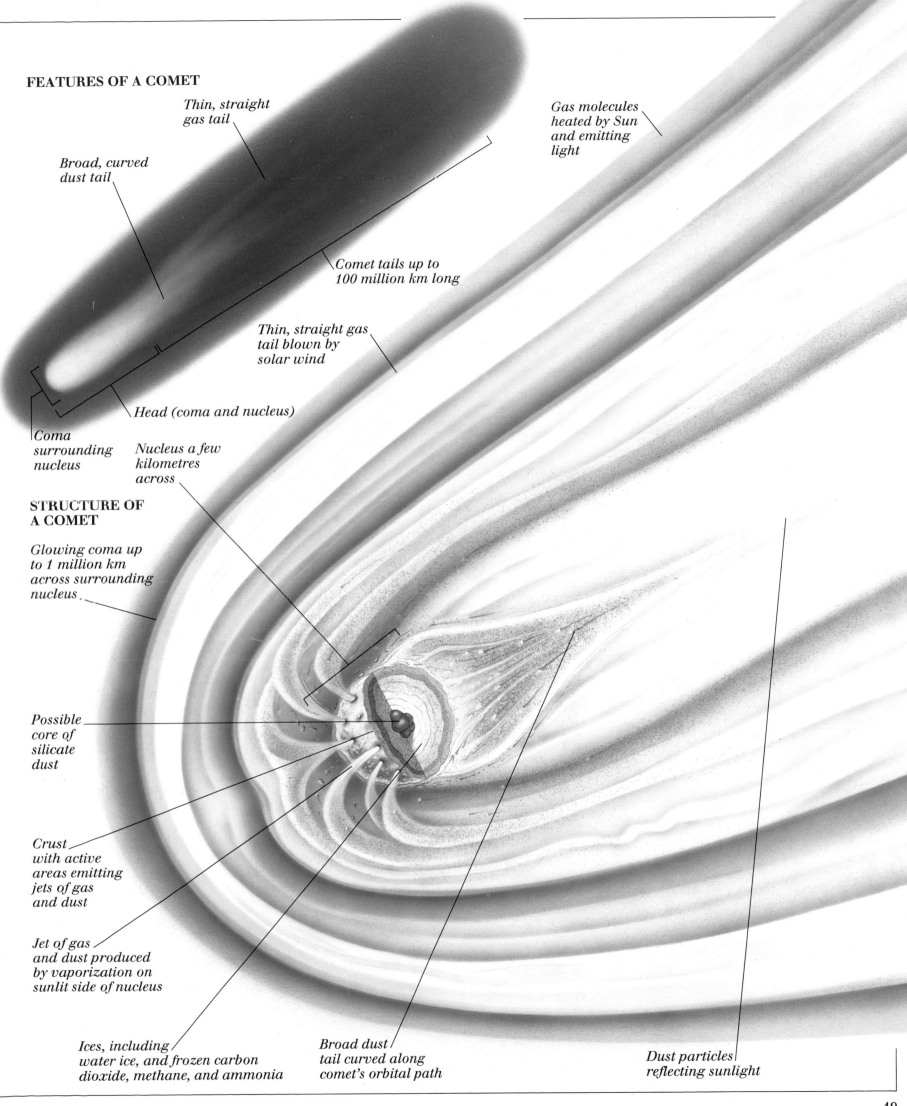

FEATURES OF A COMET

Thin, straight gas tail

Broad, curved dust tail

Gas molecules heated by Sun and emitting light

Comet tails up to 100 million km long

Thin, straight gas tail blown by solar wind

Head (coma and nucleus)

Coma surrounding nucleus

Nucleus a few kilometres across

STRUCTURE OF A COMET

Glowing coma up to 1 million km across surrounding nucleus

Possible core of silicate dust

Crust with active areas emitting jets of gas and dust

Jet of gas and dust produced by vaporization on sunlit side of nucleus

Ices, including water ice, and frozen carbon dioxide, methane, and ammonia

Broad dust tail curved along comet's orbital path

Dust particles reflecting sunlight

49

Observing space

PEOPLE HAVE ALWAYS OBSERVED the stars, but it was not until the invention of the telescope in the 17th century that it was possible to see magnified images of celestial objects. There are three main types of telescope: reflectors, refractors, and radio telescopes. Reflectors and refractors are optical telescopes: they collect and magnify visible light. Reflectors use mirrors to collect the light and refractors use lenses. The Hubble Space Telescope, which observes space from orbit, is a reflector. Space telescopes have the advantage of producing images that are undistorted by the Earth's atmosphere. Radiation from space that is absorbed by the Earth's atmosphere, such as some ultraviolet and infra-red waves, can also be detected by some space telescopes. Radio telescopes collect radio waves emitted by celestial bodies and convert them into electrical signals, which may then be used to produce images. Since the late 1950s, space probes have explored the Solar System. In 1971, the Soviet probe Mars 3 orbited Mars, transmitted pictures, and landed a capsule on the surface (although a dust storm rendered the capsule's instruments inactive). The US Viking probes to Mars were more sophisticated: they obtained weather data, photographed the terrain, and tested the soil. The US probe Voyager 2 has observed Jupiter, Saturn, Uranus, and Neptune and will continue to transmit data as it travels out of the Solar System.

RADIO TELESCOPE

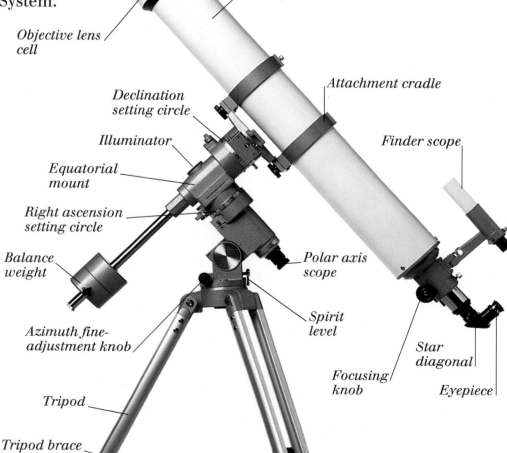

High-gain aerial

Aperture door

Primary mirror housing

Forward shell

Solar panel

Light shield

Aft shell

Access panel

Crew handrail

Equipment box

HOW TELESCOPES WORK

REFRACTOR

Objective lens

Telescope tube

Incident light ray

Refracted light ray

Eyepiece lens

REFLECTOR

Incident light ray

Eyepiece lens

Telescope tube

Primary mirror

Secondary mirror

Reflected light ray

SMALL REFRACTOR TELESCOPE

Telescope tube

Objective lens cell

Attachment cradle

Declination setting circle

Finder scope

Illuminator

Equatorial mount

Right ascension setting circle

Polar axis scope

Balance weight

Spirit level

Azimuth fine-adjustment knob

Star diagonal

Tripod

Focusing knob

Eyepiece

Tripod brace

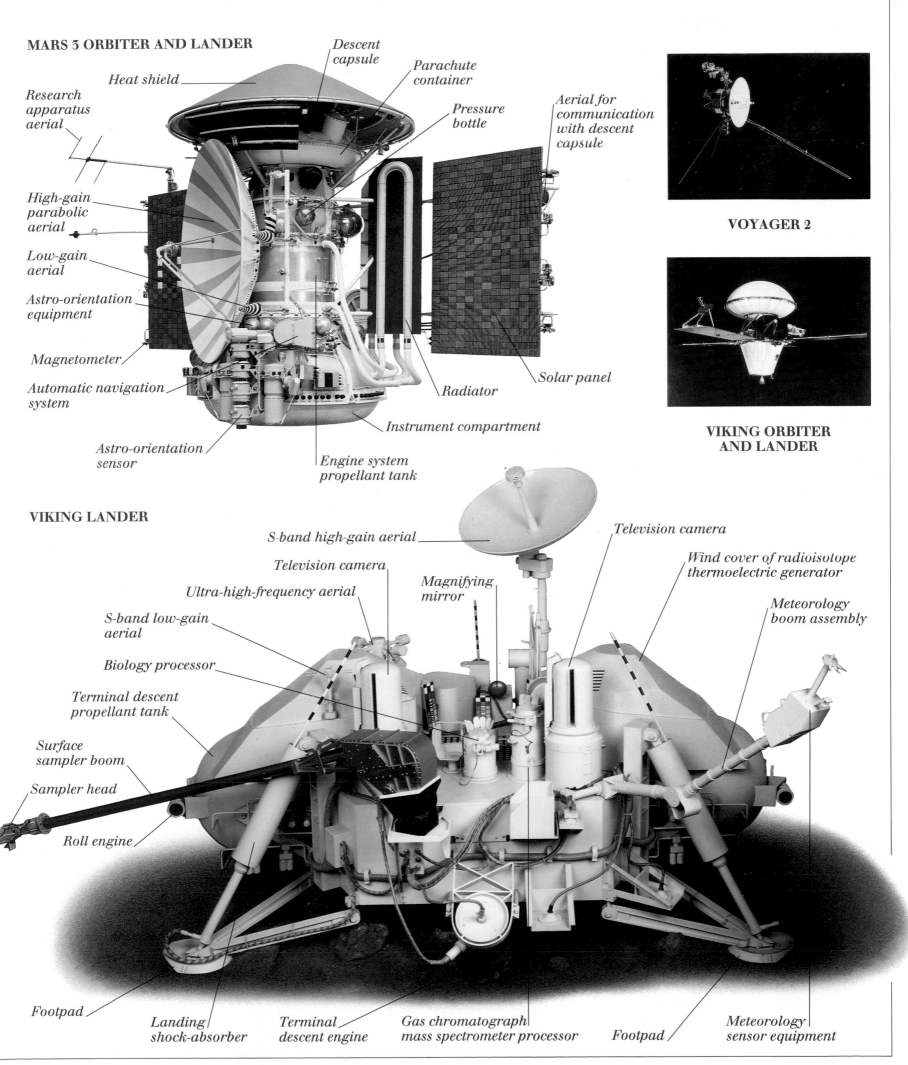

MARS 3 ORBITER AND LANDER

Heat shield

Research apparatus aerial

High-gain parabolic aerial

Low-gain aerial

Astro-orientation equipment

Magnetometer

Automatic navigation system

Astro-orientation sensor

Descent capsule

Parachute container

Pressure bottle

Aerial for communication with descent capsule

Solar panel

Radiator

Instrument compartment

Engine system propellant tank

VOYAGER 2

VIKING ORBITER AND LANDER

VIKING LANDER

S-band high-gain aerial

Television camera

Ultra-high-frequency aerial

S-band low-gain aerial

Biology processor

Terminal descent propellant tank

Surface sampler boom

Sampler head

Roll engine

Footpad

Landing shock-absorber

Terminal descent engine

Television camera

Magnifying mirror

Wind cover of radioisotope thermoelectric generator

Meteorology boom assembly

Gas chromatograph mass spectrometer processor

Footpad

Meteorology sensor equipment

Manned space exploration

THE FIRST PERSON IN SPACE was the Soviet cosmonaut, Yuri Gagarin, who completed one orbit of the Earth in his capsule Vostok 1 on 12 April 1961. For astronauts to survive in the hostile conditions of space they must be provided with an artificial environment inside a spacesuit or spacecraft. Artificial environments provide astronauts with pressure and a breathable atmosphere, protect them from radiation and micrometeoroids, and regulate their body temperature. When exploring open space or the lunar surface, astronauts connect a portable life-support system (PLSS) to their spacesuit. The US Space Shuttle is probably the most significant recent development in manned space exploration because it is reusable. Only the external fuel tank is lost on each mission; the solid rocket boosters are retrieved, and the orbiter glides back to Earth. The Shuttle has a large cargo bay, and a remote-controlled robotic arm that is used to launch, retrieve, and repair satellites in space. The cargo bay can carry a spacelab or components for a space station. Space stations have also played an important role in the recent manned exploration of space, and the development of space stations such as Skylab (US) and Mir (USSR) has shown that astronauts can live and work in space for months or even years. The US Apollo lunar missions demonstrated that it is feasible to send humans to the Moon (see pp. 54-55). The next step is to send manned spacecraft to explore the planets, although it may take decades for this to be achieved.

SPACE SHUTTLE LIFT-OFF

VOSTOK 1

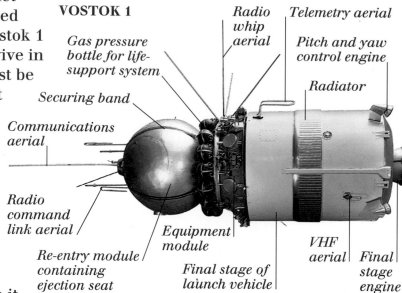

Radio whip aerial

Telemetry aerial

Gas pressure bottle for life-support system

Pitch and yaw control engine

Radiator

Securing band

Communications aerial

Radio command link aerial

Equipment module

Re-entry module containing ejection seat

Final stage of launch vehicle

VHF aerial

Final stage engine

SPACE SHUTTLE IN FLIGHT

SPACE SHUTTLE

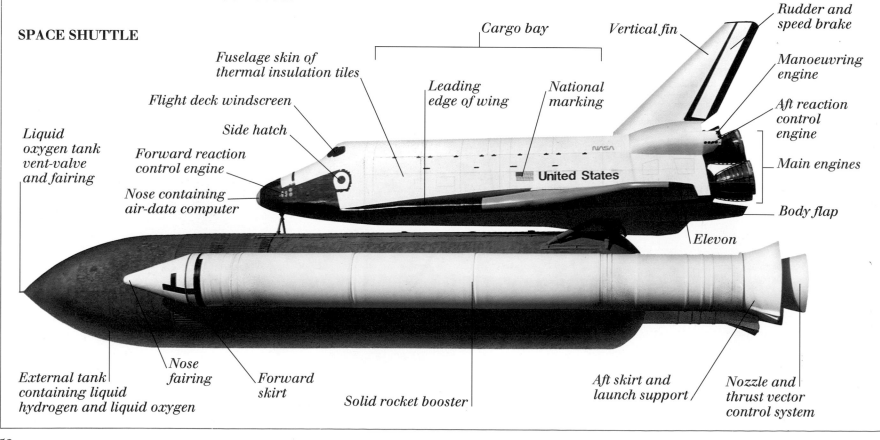

Cargo bay

Vertical fin

Rudder and speed brake

Fuselage skin of thermal insulation tiles

Leading edge of wing

National marking

Manoeuvring engine

Flight deck windscreen

Aft reaction control engine

Side hatch

Forward reaction control engine

Liquid oxygen tank vent-valve and fairing

Nose containing air-data computer

Main engines

United States

Body flap

Elevon

External tank containing liquid hydrogen and liquid oxygen

Nose fairing

Forward skirt

Solid rocket booster

Aft skirt and launch support

Nozzle and thrust vector control system

SPACESUITS

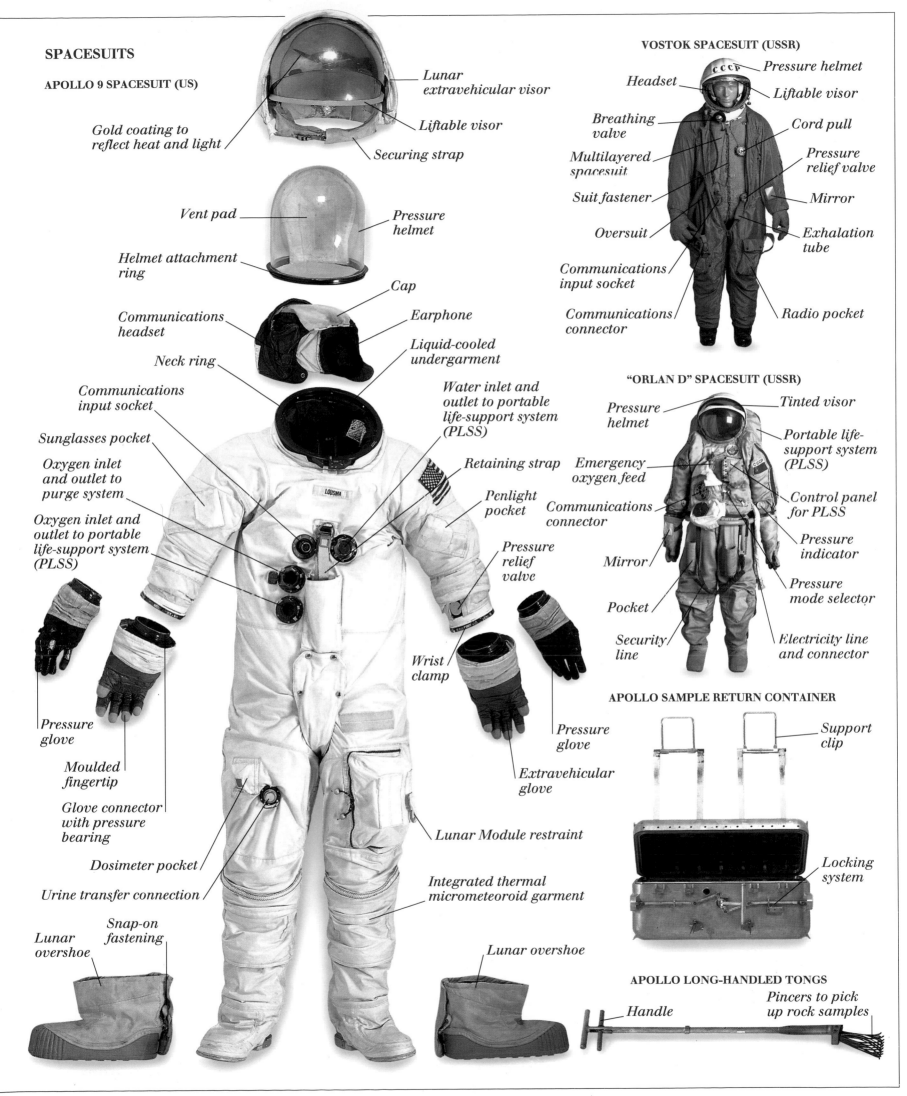

APOLLO 9 SPACESUIT (US)

Lunar extravehicular visor

Gold coating to reflect heat and light

Liftable visor

Securing strap

Vent pad

Pressure helmet

Helmet attachment ring

Cap

Communications headset

Earphone

Neck ring

Liquid-cooled undergarment

Communications input socket

Water inlet and outlet to portable life-support system (PLSS)

Sunglasses pocket

Retaining strap

Oxygen inlet and outlet to purge system

Penlight pocket

Oxygen inlet and outlet to portable life-support system (PLSS)

Pressure relief valve

Pressure glove

Moulded fingertip

Wrist clamp

Pressure glove

Glove connector with pressure bearing

Extravehicular glove

Dosimeter pocket

Lunar Module restraint

Urine transfer connection

Integrated thermal micrometeoroid garment

Snap-on fastening

Lunar overshoe

Lunar overshoe

VOSTOK SPACESUIT (USSR)

Pressure helmet

Headset

Liftable visor

Breathing valve

Cord pull

Multilayered spacesuit

Pressure relief valve

Suit fastener

Mirror

Oversuit

Exhalation tube

Communications input socket

Communications connector

Radio pocket

"ORLAN D" SPACESUIT (USSR)

Pressure helmet

Tinted visor

Portable life-support system (PLSS)

Emergency oxygen feed

Control panel for PLSS

Communications connector

Pressure indicator

Mirror

Pressure mode selector

Pocket

Electricity line and connector

Security line

APOLLO SAMPLE RETURN CONTAINER

Support clip

Locking system

APOLLO LONG-HANDLED TONGS

Handle

Pincers to pick up rock samples

Lunar exploration

APOLLO 11 LIFT-OFF

THE MOON IS THE NEAREST celestial body to Earth, yet until relatively recently little was known about it. Extensive exploration was first undertaken by unmanned probes. The Soviet Luna 2 was the first probe to reach the Moon, in 1959, and in 1966 Luna 9 transmitted the first pictures from the surface. One of the most sophisticated unmanned lunar probes was the remote-controlled Soviet vehicle Lunokhod 1, which travelled over the lunar surface taking television pictures and testing the soil. The first men landed on the Moon as part of the US Apollo 11 mission on 20 July 1969. Apollo 11 had three components: a command module, a service module, and a lunar module. After going into orbit round the Moon, the lunar module descended to the Moon's surface with two astronauts (Neil Armstrong and Edwin "Buzz" Aldrin) on board. The astronauts collected rock samples, took photographs, and set up research equipment. They took off from the Moon in the module's ascent stage and docked with the command module before travelling the 384,400 kilometres back to Earth. A further 10 US astronauts explored the Moon before the Apollo programme ended in 1972. Since then, only a small number of unmanned spacecraft have landed on the Moon.

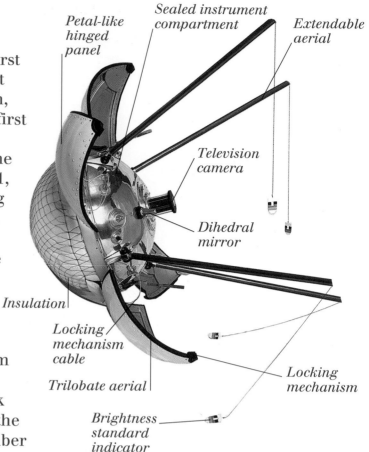

Petal-like hinged panel

Sealed instrument compartment

Extendable aerial

Television camera

Dihedral mirror

Insulation

Locking mechanism cable

Trilobate aerial

Locking mechanism

Brightness standard indicator

LUNOKHOD 1

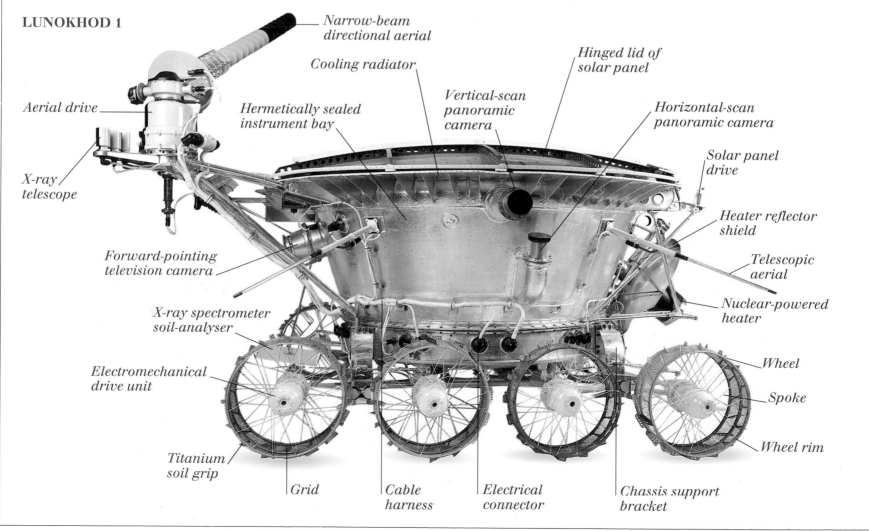

Narrow-beam directional aerial

Cooling radiator

Hinged lid of solar panel

Vertical-scan panoramic camera

Horizontal-scan panoramic camera

Aerial drive

Hermetically sealed instrument bay

Solar panel drive

X-ray telescope

Heater reflector shield

Telescopic aerial

Forward-pointing television camera

Nuclear-powered heater

X-ray spectrometer soil-analyser

Wheel

Electromechanical drive unit

Spoke

Titanium soil grip

Wheel rim

Grid

Cable harness

Electrical connector

Chassis support bracket

54

APOLLO 16 LUNAR MODULE

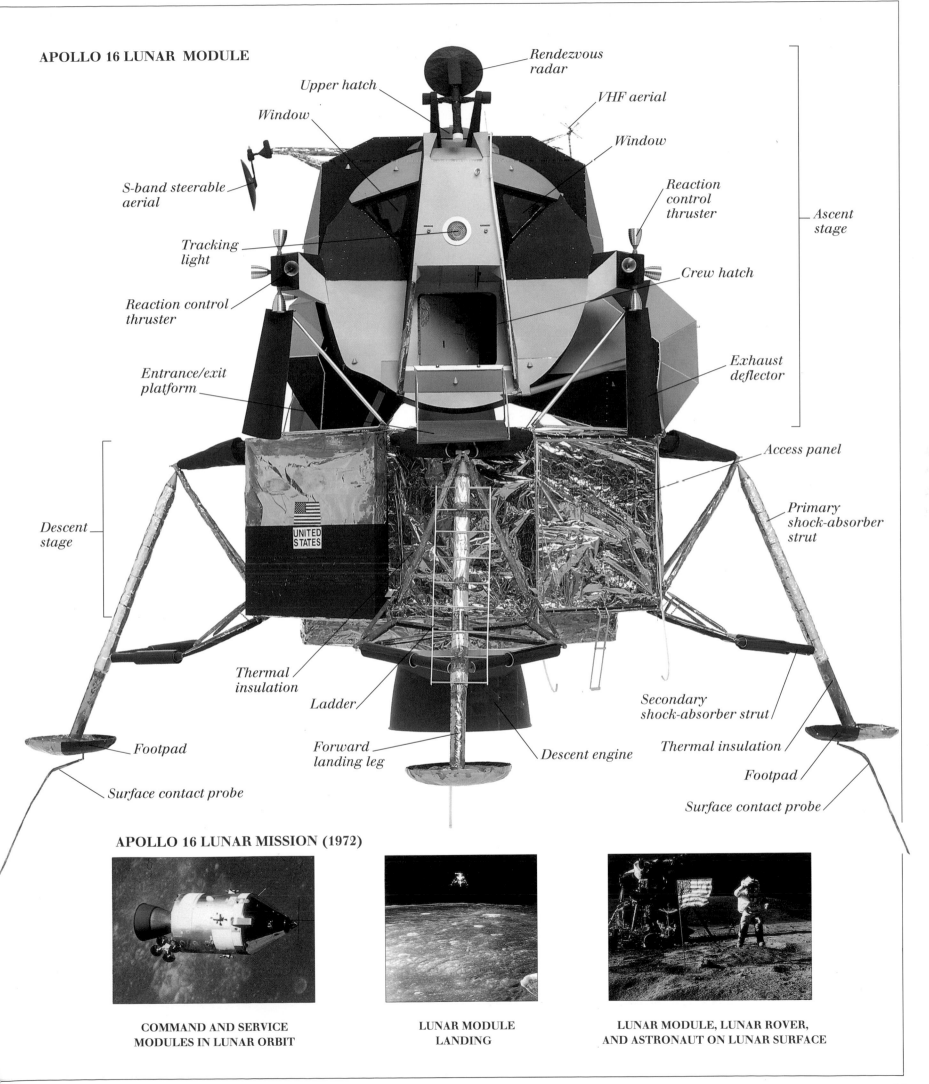

Rendezvous radar

Upper hatch

Window

VHF aerial

Window

S-band steerable aerial

Reaction control thruster

Tracking light

Ascent stage

Crew hatch

Reaction control thruster

Entrance/exit platform

Exhaust deflector

Access panel

Descent stage

Primary shock-absorber strut

UNITED STATES

Thermal insulation

Secondary shock-absorber strut

Footpad

Ladder

Thermal insulation

Surface contact probe

Forward landing leg

Descent engine

Footpad

Surface contact probe

APOLLO 16 LUNAR MISSION (1972)

COMMAND AND SERVICE MODULES IN LUNAR ORBIT

LUNAR MODULE LANDING

LUNAR MODULE, LUNAR ROVER, AND ASTRONAUT ON LUNAR SURFACE

Astronomical data 1

PLANETS OF THE SOLAR SYSTEM

Mercury Venus Earth Mars Jupiter Saturn Uranus Neptune Pluto

PLANETS

	Mercury	Venus	Earth	Mars	Jupiter	Saturn	Uranus	Neptune	Pluto
Mass (Earth = 1)	0.055	0.81	1	0.11	318	95.18	14.5	17.14	0.0022
Equatorial diameter (km)	4,878	12,103	12,756	6,786	142,984	120,536	51,118	49,528	2,300
Volume (Earth = 1)	0.056	0.86	1	0.15	1,323	744	67	57	unknown
Average density (g/cm³; water = 1g/cm³)	5.42	5.25	5.52	3.94	1.33	0.69	1.27	1.71	2.03
Equatorial surface gravity (Earth = 1)	0.38	0.86	1	0.38	2.5	1.1	1.1	1.1	unknown
Equatorial escape velocity (km/sec)	4.3	10.3	11.2	5	59.5	35.6	21.2	23.6	1.1
Axial tilt (degrees)	2	2	23.4	24	3.1	26.7	97.9	28.8	57.5
Rotational period (length of day) (d = Earth day, h = Earth hour)	58.65d	243.01d*	23.93h	24.62h	9.92h	10.67h	17.23h*	16.12h	6.38d*
Average surface temperature (°C)	-170 to 430	464	15	-40	-120	-180	-210	-220	-220
Number of known rings	0	0	0	0	1	7	11	4	0
Number of moons	0	0	1	2	16	18	15	8	1
Maximum apparent magnitude	-1.4	-4.4	-	-2.8	-2.8	-0.3	5.5	7.8	13.6
Aphelion (million km)	69.7	109	152.1	249.1	815.7	1,507	3,004	4,537	7,375
Perihelion (million km)	45.9	107.4	147.1	206.7	740.9	1,347	2,735	4,456	4,425
Average distance from Sun (million km)	57.9	108.2	149.6	227.9	778.3	1,427	2,869.6	4,496.6	5,900
Average orbital velocity (km/sec)	47.89	35.03	29.79	24.13	13.06	9.64	6.81	5.43	4.74
Orbital tilt (degrees)	7	3.39	0	1.85	1.3	2.49	0.77	1.77	17.2
Orbital period (length of year) (y = Earth year, d = Earth day)	87.97d	224.7d	365.26d	1.88y	11.86y	29.46y	84.01y	164.79y	248.54y

*= rotation is retrograde

THE SUN

Approximate age (billion years)	4.6
Star type	Yellow main sequence
Mass (Earth = 1)	332,946
Equatorial diameter (km)	1,392,000
Average density (g/cm³; water = 1g/cm³)	1.41
Apparent magnitude	-26.7
Absolute magnitude	4.83
Luminosity (billion billion megawatts)	390
Average surface temperature (°C)	5,500
Approximate core temperature (°C)	15,000,000
Maximum distance from Earth (km)	152,000,000
Minimum distance from Earth (km)	147,000,000
Average distance from Earth (km)	149,600,000
Polar rotation period (Earth days)	35
Equatorial rotation period (Earth days)	25

FAMOUS COMETS

Name	Period (years)
D'Arrest's Comet	6.6
Encke's Comet	3.3
Comet Giacobini-Zinner	6.5
Great Comet of 1811	3,000
Great Comet of 1843	512.4
Great Comet of 1844	102,050
Great Comet of 1864	2,800,000
Halley's Comet	76.3
Holmes' Comet	6.9
Comet Kohoutek	75,000
Comet Mrkós	5.3
Olber's Comet	74
Pons-Winnecke Comet	6
Comet Schwassmann-Wachmann	16.2

COMET

MOONS

Name of planet	Name of moon	Diameter (km)	Average distance from planet (km)	Orbital period (Earth days)	Orbital tilt (degrees)
Earth	Moon	3,476	384,400	27.3	5.1
Mars	Phobos	22*	9,400	0.3	1.1
	Deimos	13*	23,500	1.4	1.8
Jupiter	Metis	40	128,000	0.3	0
	Adrastea	20*	129,000	0.3	0
	Amalthea	200	181,300	0.5	0.45
	Thebe	100*	221,900	0.7	0.9
	Io	3,642	421,800	1.8	0.04
	Europa	3,138	670,900	3.6	0.47
	Ganymede	5,262	1,070,000	7.2	0.21
	Callisto	4,800	1,880,000	16.7	0.51
	Leda	15	11,094,000	238.7	26.1
	Himalia	170	11,480,000	250.6	27.6
	Lysithea	35	11,720,000	259.2	29
	Elara	70	11,737,000	259	24.8
	Ananke	25	21,200,000	631	147
	Carme	40	22,600,000	692	164
	Pasiphae	60	23,500,000	735	145
	Sinope	40	23,700,000	758	153
Saturn	Pan	20	133,600	0.57	very small
	Atlas	31*	137,700	0.6	0.3
	Prometheus	102*	139,400	0.6	0
	Pandora	85*	141,700	0.6	0.1
	Epimetheus	117	151,400	0.7	0.3
	Janus	188*	151,500	0.7	0.1
	Mimas	397	186,000	0.9	1.52
	Enceladus	498	238,000	1.4	0.02
	Tethys	1,050	295,000	1.9	1.86
	Telesto	22*	295,000	1.9	unknown
	Calypso	24*	295,000	1.9	unknown
	Dione	1,118	377,000	2.7	0.02
	Helene	32*	377,000	2.7	0.2
	Rhea	1,528	527,000	4.6	0.35
	Titan	5,150	1,222,000	15.9	0.33
	Hyperion	286*	1,481,100	21.3	0.43
	Iapetus	1,436	3,561,300	79.3	14.7
	Phoebe	220	12,954,000	550.4	175
Uranus	Cordelia	26	49,700	0.3	very small
	Ophelia	32	53,800	0.4	very small
	Bianca	44	59,200	0.4	very small
	Cressida	66	61,800	0.5	very small
	Desdemona	58	62,700	0.5	very small
	Juliet	84	64,400	0.5	very small
	Portia	110	66,100	0.5	very small
	Rosalind	58	69,900	0.6	very small
	Belinda	68	75,300	0.6	very small
	Puck	154	86,000	0.8	very small
	Miranda	472	129,800	1.4	3.4
	Ariel	1,158	191,200	2.5	0
	Umbriel	1,169	266,000	4.1	0
	Titania	1,578	435,900	8.7	0
	Oberon	1,523	582,600	13.5	0
Neptune	Naiad	54	48,000	0.3	0
	Thalassa	80	50,000	0.3	0
	Despina	180	52,500	0.3	0
	Galatea	150	62,000	0.4	0
	Larissa	192	73,600	0.6	0
	Proteus	416	117,600	1.1	4.5
	Triton	2,705	354,800	5.9	160
	Nereid	300	5,514,000	360.2	27
Pluto	Charon	1,200	19,600	6.4	98.8

*= average diameter for irregularly shaped moon

THE MOON

TOTAL SOLAR ECLIPSES (UNTIL 2005)

Date	Where visible
3 November 1994	Indian Ocean, South Atlantic, South America, Mid-Pacific.
24 October 1995	Middle East, South Asia, South Pacific.
9 March 1997	Siberia, Arctic.
26 February 1998	Mid-Pacific, Central America, North Atlantic.
11 August 1999	North Atlantic, North Europe, Middle East, North India.
21 June 2001	South America, South Atlantic, Southern Africa, Pacific.
4 December 2002	Mid-Atlantic, Southern Africa, South Pacific, Australia.
23 November 2003	South Pacific, Antarctica.

TOTAL LUNAR ECLIPSES (UNTIL 2005)

Date	Where visible
29 November 1993	North, South, and Central America.
4 April 1996	Africa, South-east Europe.
27 September 1996	North, South, and Central America, West Africa.
16 September 1997	Southern Africa, East Africa, Australia.
21 January 2000	North, South, and Central America, South-west Europe, West Africa.
16 July 2000	Pacific, Australia, South-east Asia.
9 January 2001	Africa, Asia, Europe.
16 May 2003	South and Central America, Antarctica.
9 November 2003	North, South, and Central America.
4 May 2004	Africa, Middle East, India.
28 October 2004	North, South, and Central America, West Africa, South Europe.

Astronomical data 2

LOCAL GROUP OF GALAXIES

Name/Catalogue number	Type	Distance (light years)	Luminosity (million Suns)	Diameter (light years)
Milky Way	Spiral	0	15,000	100,000
Large Magellanic Cloud	Irregular spiral	170,000	2,000	30,000
Small Magellanic Cloud	Irregular	190,000	500	20,000
Sculptor	Elliptical	300,000	1	6,000
Carina	Elliptical	300,000	0.01	3,000
Draco	Elliptical	300,000	0.1	3,000
Sextans	Elliptical	300,000	0.01	3,000
Ursa Minor	Elliptical	300,000	0.1	2,000
Fornax	Elliptical	500,000	12	6,000
Leo I	Elliptical	600,000	0.6	2,000
Leo II	Elliptical	600,000	0.4	2,000
NGC 6822	Irregular	1,800,000	90	15,000
IC 5152	Irregular	2,000,000	60	3,000
WLM	Irregular	2,000,000	90	6,000
Andromeda (M31)	Spiral	2,200,000	40,000	150,000
Andromeda I	Elliptical	2,200,000	1	5,000
Andromeda II	Elliptical	2,200,000	1	5,000
Andromeda III	Elliptical	2,200,000	1	5,000
M32 (NGC 221)	Elliptical	2,200,000	130	5,000
NGC 147	Elliptical	2,200,000	50	8,000
NGC 185	Elliptical	2,200,000	60	8,000
NGC 205	Elliptical	2,200,000	160	11,000
M33 (Triangulum)	Spiral	2,400,000	5,000	40,000
IC 1613	Irregular	2,500,000	50	10,000
DDO 210	Irregular	3,000,000	2	5,000
Pisces	Irregular	3,000,000	0.6	2,000
GR 8	Irregular	4,000,000	2	1,500
IC 10	Irregular	4,000,000	250	6,000
Sagittarius	Irregular	4,000,000	1	4,000
Leo A	Irregular	5,000,000	20	7,000
Pegasus	Irregular	5,000,000	20	7,000

SIDE VIEW OF OUR GALAXY (THE MILKY WAY)

OVERHEAD VIEW OF OUR GALAXY (THE MILKY WAY)

BRIGHTEST STARS

Name/Catalogue number	Constellation	Apparent magnitude	Absolute magnitude	Distance (light years)	Star type
Sun		-26.7	4.8	0.000015*	Yellow main sequence
Sirius A	Canis Major (The Great Dog)	-1.4	1.4	8.6	White main sequence
Canopus	Carina (The Keel)	-0.7	-8.5	1,200	White supergiant
Alpha Centauri A	Centaurus (The Centaur)	-0.1	4.1	4.3	Yellow main sequence
Arcturus	Boötes (The Herdsman)	-0.1	-0.3	37	Red giant
Vega	Lyra (The Lyre)	0.04	0.5	27	White main sequence
Capella	Auriga (The Charioteer)	0.1	-0.6	45	Yellow giant
Rigel	Orion (The Huntsman)	0.1	-7.1	540–900	White supergiant
Procyon	Canis Minor (The Little Dog)	0.4	2.7	11.3	Yellow main sequence
Achernar	Eridanus (River Eridanus)	0.5	-1.3	85	White main sequence

*= 149,600,000 km

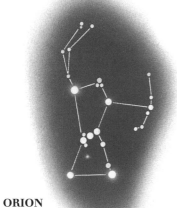

ORION

NEAREST STARS

Name/Catalogue number	Constellation	Distance (light years)	Apparent magnitude	Absolute magnitude	Star type
Sun		0.000015*	-26.7	4.8	Yellow main sequence
Proxima Centauri	Centaurus (The Centaur)	4.2	11	15.5	Red dwarf
Alpha Centauri A	Centaurus (The Centaur)	4.3	-0.1	4.1	Yellow main sequence
Alpha Centauri B	Centaurus (The Centaur)	4.3	1.4	5.7	Orange main sequence
Barnard's Star	Ophiuchus (The Serpent Bearer)	5.9	9.5	13	Red dwarf
Wolf 359	Leo (The Lion)	7.6	13.5	16.7	Red dwarf
Lalande 21185	Ursa Major (The Great Bear)	8.1	7.5	10.4	Red dwarf
Sirius A	Canis Major (The Great Dog)	8.6	-1.4	1.5	White main sequence
Sirius B	Canis Major (The Great Dog)	8.6	8.7	12	White dwarf
UV Ceti A	Cetus (The Whale)	8.9	12.4	15	Red dwarf

*= 149,600,000 km

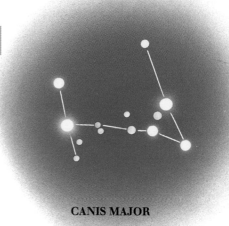

CANIS MAJOR

Glossary

ACCRETION DISC: A disc of material spiralling around an object, such as a black hole, due to gravity.

APHELION: The point furthest from the Sun in the orbit of a body around the Sun. (See also Perihelion.)

APOGEE: The point furthest from the Earth in the orbit of the Moon or an artificial satellite around the Earth. (See also Perigee.)

ASTEROID (MINOR PLANET): A small, rocky body orbiting the Sun, usually in the asteroid belt between Mars and Jupiter.

ASTRONOMICAL UNIT (AU): A unit of distance equal to the average distance between the Earth and the Sun: 149,597,870 km.

ATMOSPHERE: The outer gaseous layer around a planet, moon, or star. It has no definite outer boundary and thins out until it merges into space.

AXIS OF ROTATION: The imaginary line about which a body rotates. The **axial tilt** or **inclination** is the angle between the axis of rotation and the perpendicular to the orbital plane. (See also Orbit.)

BIG BANG THEORY: The theory that the Universe began when space, time, and matter came into being in a huge explosion (the Big Bang) between 10 and 20 billion years ago.

BINARY STAR: A pair of stars that orbit one another. About half of all known stars belong to groups of two or more.

BLACK HOLE: A region of space around a collapsed star where gravity is so strong that nothing, not even light, can escape. (See also Event horizon.)

CELESTIAL SPHERE: An imaginary hollow sphere on which, from the Earth, celestial objects appear to lie. The **celestial equator** is marked by the projection of the Earth's equator on to the celestial sphere. The **celestial poles** are the points on the celestial sphere above the Earth's north and south poles.

COMET: A small, icy body orbiting the Sun in a long, eccentric orbit.

CONSTELLATION: The pattern formed by a group of stars in the sky. The stars are not necessarily physically associated, since they may lie at different distances from the Earth.

DAY: The time taken for a planet to rotate once about its axis. A **sidereal day** is the time taken for a star to return to the same position in the sky. A **solar day** lasts from sunrise to sunrise.

DWARF STAR: A main sequence star (see Main sequence star).

ECLIPSE: The total or partial obscuring of one celestial body by another. In a **solar eclipse**, the Moon passes between the Sun and the Earth, hiding part or all of the Sun from a small area on Earth. In a

lunar eclipse, the Earth comes between the Moon and the Sun, and the Moon passes through the Earth's shadow.

ECLIPTIC: The plane in which the Earth orbits around the Sun.

EVENT HORIZON: The boundary of a black hole. Light emitted from inside the event horizon cannot escape, so it is impossible to observe events occurring within it. (See also Black hole.)

GALAXY: A collection of stars, gas, and dust held together by gravity. Galaxies are classified as **spiral**, **elliptical**, or **irregular** according to their shape. They usually occur in groups known as **clusters**.

GIANT AND SUPERGIANT STARS: Large stars with a high luminosity. **Giants** are 10–1,000 times brighter than the Sun, with diameters 10–100 times greater. **Supergiants** are the largest and most luminous stars, thousands of times brighter and with diameters up to 1,000 times greater than the Sun.

GRAVITATION (GRAVITY): The attractive force between bodies, which depends on their mass and the distance between them. It holds less massive bodies in orbit around more massive ones, such as the planets around the Sun.

HERTZSPRUNG-RUSSELL DIAGRAM: A graph displaying the relationship between the luminosities and spectral types (colours) of stars. Other factors, such as stellar temperature, may also be included.

LIGHT YEAR: A unit of distance equal to the distance travelled by light (or any electromagnetic radiation) through a vacuum in one year. One light year is 9.46 million million km, or 63,240 astronomical units, or 0.3066 parsecs. One **light second** is 299,792 km. (See also Astronomical unit; Parsec.)

LOCAL GROUP OF GALAXIES: The cluster of at least 28 galaxies to which our galaxy (the Milky Way Galaxy) belongs.

LUMINOSITY: The brightness of a luminous body, e.g., a star, defined by the total energy it radiates in a given time.

MAGNITUDE: A measurement of the brightness of a star or other celestial body. **Apparent magnitude** is the brightness of an object as seen from Earth. **Absolute magnitude** is the magnitude that an object would have if observed from a standard distance of 10 parsecs. (See also Luminosity.)

MAIN SEQUENCE STAR: A star that falls within a well-defined diagonal band on the Hertzsprung-Russell diagram. Main sequence stars produce energy by fusing hydrogen to form helium in their cores. (See also Hertzsprung-Russell diagram.)

METEOROID: A particle of dust or rock travelling through space at high speed. A **meteor** (also called a shooting star) is the streak of light seen when a meteoroid burns up in the Earth's atmosphere. A

meteorite is a larger meteoroid that enters the atmosphere and reaches the surface of the Earth. **Meteor showers** occur when the Earth passes through a stream of debris in space.

MILKY WAY: The band of hazy light across the night sky coming from the multitude of stars in our galaxy.

MOON: A natural satellite of a planet. Also the name for the Earth's only natural satellite. (See also Satellite.)

NEBULA: A cloud of interstellar gas and dust. Nebulae are detectable as **emission nebulae**, which glow, **reflection nebulae**, which scatter starlight, and **dark nebulae**, which obscure light from more distant stars or nebulae.

NEUTRINO: An elementary particle with no electric charge and almost no mass, effectively travelling at the speed of light. Neutrinos very rarely interact with any other matter.

NEUTRON STAR: A stellar core that has collapsed until it consists almost entirely of neutrons. It has a mass between about 1.5 and 3 solar masses, but a very small diameter (typically about 10 km). Neutron stars are detected as pulsars (see Pulsar).

ORBIT: The curved path of a body through space, influenced by the gravitational pull of a more massive body. The **orbital plane** is the plane in which the orbit lies. The **orbital tilt** is the angle between the orbital plane and a reference plane, e.g., the ecliptic. The **orbital period** is the time a body takes to complete one orbit. (See also Year; Ecliptic.)

PARSEC: A unit of distance equal to 3.26 light years, or 206,265 astronomical units. (See also Astronomical unit; Light year.)

PERIGEE: The point nearest the Earth in the orbit of the Moon or an artificial satellite around the Earth. (See also Apogee.)

PERIHELION: The point nearest the Sun in the orbit of a planet or other body around the Sun. (See also Aphelion.)

PHASES: The apparent changes in shape of the Moon and some planets as different amounts of their sunlit sides become visible from Earth.

PLANET: A relatively large body in orbit around the Sun or another star. Planets shine only by reflecting light.

PROTOSTAR: The earliest stage in the life of a star, during which it is condensing in a nebula but before it becomes a main sequence star.

PULSAR: A source of regularly pulsating radio waves (and sometimes light and other radiation). Pulsars are believed to be rotating neutron stars.

QUASAR (QUASI-STELLAR OBJECT): A compact, extremely luminous object that appears like a star when viewed from Earth. Little is known about quasars, but

they are probably the nuclei of active galaxies, with supermassive black holes as their energy source.

RADIATION: Waves or particles emitted by a source. **Electromagnetic radiation** is energy travelling in the form of waves, including gamma rays, X-rays, ultraviolet radiation, visible light, infra-red radiation, microwaves, and radio waves. **Particle radiation** includes elementary particles such as the protons and electrons in the solar wind.

RED DWARF: A small star with low surface temperature, and the faintest luminosity of all main sequence stars (see Main sequence star).

RETROGRADE MOTION: Backwards motion, i.e., clockwise motion (viewed from above) of a body around the Sun, or of a moon around its planet, or of a planet around its axis of rotation.

RING SYSTEM: A thin disc of dust, rocks, or ice particles orbiting in the equatorial plane of some large planets.

SATELLITE: A body in orbit around a larger, parent body. **Natural satellites** of planets are called moons. **Artificial satellites** have been put into orbit around the Earth, the Moon, and some other planets. (See also Moon.)

SINGULARITY: A theoretical point or region in space-time where the laws of physics break down. Theory predicts a singularity with infinite density and pressure at the centre of a black hole.

SOLAR SYSTEM: The Sun and all the bodies that orbit around it due to gravity.

SPECTRUM: A band or series of lines of electromagnetic radiation produced by splitting the radiation into its constituent wavelengths, e.g., the band of rainbow colours produced by splitting white light.

STAR: A luminous ball of gas that shines by generating energy in its core by nuclear reactions.

SUN: The central star of the Solar System. It is a main sequence star and is average in size and luminosity.

SUPERNOVA: The catastrophic explosion of a massive star at the end of its life, during which it may become as bright as a whole galaxy. A **supernova remnant** is the expanding cloud it leaves behind.

VARIABLE STAR: A star whose brightness varies.

WHITE DWARF: A small, very dense, collapsed star that is gradually cooling.

YEAR: The time taken for a planet to orbit the Sun once. A **sidereal year** is the time for one orbit measured using the fixed stars as a positional reference point. A **tropical year** is one orbit measured using a specific position of the Sun on the celestial sphere as a reference point. (See also Celestial sphere; Orbit.)

Index

A

51 Andromedae 15
Absolute magnitude
    Brightest stars 58
    Hertzsprung-Russell
        diagram 19
    Nearest stars 58
    Stars 18
    Sun 56
Absorption lines 18-19
Acamar 15
Access panel
    Apollo 16 55
    Hubble Space Telescope 50
Accretion disc 59
    Life of massive star 23
    Neutron stars and black
        holes 24-25
Achernar
    Brightest stars 58
    Southern stars 16
Acidalia Planitia 39
Acrux
    Centaurus and Crux 17
    Southern stars 17
Active galaxies 8
Adams ring
    Neptune's rings 46
    Structure of Neptune 47
Adhara
    Canis Major 17
    Northern stars 14
    Southern stars 17
Adrastea 57
Aerial 51
Aerial drive 54
Africa
    Satellite views of Earth 34
    Structure of Earth 35
African plate 34
Aino Planitia
    Radar map of Venus 32
    Structure of Venus 33
Akna Montes 33
Alba Fossae 39
Alba Patera 39
Albategnius 36
Albireo 16
Alcor 15
Alcyone 16
Aldebaran
    Northern stars 14
    Southern stars 17
Alderamin 15
Aldrin, Edwin "Buzz" 54
Algedi 16
Algenib
    Northern stars 15
    Pegasus and Andromeda 15
    Southern stars 16
Algieba 14
Algol
    Northern stars 15
    Southern stars 16
Alhena
    Northern stars 14
    Southern stars 17
Alioth
    Northern stars 14
    The Plough 15
Alkaid
    Northern stars 14
    The Plough 15
Almach
    Northern stars 15
    Pegasus and Andromeda 15
    Southern stars 16
Al Nair
    Northern stars 15
    Southern stars 16
Alnilam 14
Alnitak
    Horsehead Nebula 12
    Orion 14
Alpha Centauri 17
Alpha Centauri A
    Brightest stars 58
    Nearest stars 58

Alpha Centauri B 58
Alpha Hydri 16
Alpha Mensae 16
Alphard
    Northern stars 14
    Southern stars 17
Alpha Regio
    Radar map of Venus 32
    Structure of Venus 33
Alpha ring 44
Alphecca
    Northern stars 14
    Southern stars 17
Alpheratz
    Northern stars 15
    Pegasus and Andromeda
        15
    Southern stars 16
Alphonsus 36
Alrami 17
Altair
    Northern stars 15
    Southern stars 16
Aludra 17
Amalthea 57
Amazon Basin 35
Amazonis Planitia 39
Amazon River 34
Ammonia
    Jupiter's atmosphere 41
    Saturn's atmosphere 43
    Structure of Neptune 47
    Structure of Uranus 45
Ammonia crystals
    Jupiter's atmosphere 41
    Saturn's atmosphere 43
Ammonium hydrosulphide
    crystals
    Jupiter's atmosphere 41
    Saturn's atmosphere 43
Ananke 57
Anatolian plate 34
Andes
    Satellite views of Earth 34
    Structure of Earth 35
Andromeda 15
    Local Group of galaxies
        58
    Northern stars 15
    Southern stars 16
Andromeda I 58
Andromeda II 58
Andromeda III 58
Andromeda Galaxy
    Our galaxy and nearby
        galaxies 10
    Pegasus and Andromeda
        15
Anne's Spot 43
Antarctica 34
Antarctic plate 34
Antares
    Northern stars 14
    Southern stars 17
Anticyclonic storm system
    Cloud features of Neptune
        46
    Jupiter 40-41
    Structure of Saturn 43
Antlia
    Northern stars 14
    Southern stars 17
Antoniadi 37
Aperture door 50
Aphelion 59
    Planets 26-27, 56
Aphrodite Terra 32-33
Apogee 59
Apollo 37
Apollo 9 spacesuit 53
Apollo 16 lunar mission 55
Apollo long-handled tongs 53
Apollo sample return container
    53
Apparent magnitude 59
    Brightest stars 58
    Nearest stars 58
    Planets 56
    Stars 18
    Sun 56

Aquarius
    Northern stars 15
    Southern stars 16
Aquila
    Northern stars 15
    Southern stars 16
Ara 16
Arabian plate 34
Arcadia Planitia 39
Archimedes 36
Arcturus
    Brightest stars 58
    Hertzsprung-Russell
        diagram 19
    Northern stars 14
    Southern stars 17
Argon
    Earth's atmosphere 35
    Mars' atmosphere 39
    Mercury's atmosphere 31
    Venus' atmosphere 33
Argyre Planitia 39
Ariel
    Moons 57
    Uranus' moons 44
Aries
    Northern stars 15
    Southern stars 16
A ring 42-43
Aristarchus 36
Aristillus 36
Aristoteles 36
Arkab Prior 17
Armstrong, Neil 54
Arsia Mons 39
Artificial satellites 59
Arzachel 36
Ascent stage 55
Ascraeus Mons 39
Asia 34
Asteroid 951 Gaspra 48
Asteroid belt
    Asteroids, comets, and
        meteoroids 48
    Solar System 26
Asteroids 48-49, 59
    Solar System 26
Astronomical data 56-58
Astronomical unit 59
Astro-orientation equipment 51
Astro-orientation sensor 51
Atalanta Planitia 32
Atlantic Ocean 34
Atlas
    Moons 57
    Near side of the Moon 36
Atlas Mountains 35
Atmosphere 59
    Earth 35
    Jupiter 41
    Mars 39
    Mercury 30-31
    Neptune 47
    Pluto 47
    Saturn 43
    Uranus 45
    Venus 33
Atmospheric pressure 32
Attachment cradle 50
Auriga
    Brightest stars 58
    Northern stars 14
    Southern stars 17
Australia 34
Avogadro 37
Axial tilt
    Earth 34
    Jupiter 40
    Mars 38
    Mercury 30
    The Moon 36
    Neptune 46
    Planets 56
    Pluto 47
    Saturn 42
    Uranus 44
    Venus 32
Axis of rotation 59
    Earth 34
    Jupiter 40
    Mars 38
    Mercury 30
    The Moon 36
    Neptune 46
    Pluto 47
    Pulsar 24
    Saturn 42

Uranus 44
Venus 32
Azimuth fine-adjustment knob
    50

B

Bach 31
Background radiation 6
Bailly 36
Balance weight 50
Balzac 31
Barnard's Star
    Hertzsprung-Russell
        diagram 19
    Nearest stars 58
Beethoven 31
Belinda 57
Bello 31
Bell Regio
    Radar map of Venus 32
    Structure of Venus 33
Belt
    Jupiter 40-41
    Structure of Saturn 43
Beta Hydri 16
Beta Mensae 16
Beta Pictoris 17
Beta ring 44
Betelgeuse
    Hertzsprung-Russell
        diagram 19
    Northern stars 14
    Orion 14
    Southern stars 17
Bianca 57
Big Bang theory 59
    Universe 6-7
Binary star 59
Biology processor 51
Black dwarf 20-21
Black holes 24-25, 59
    Galaxies 8
    Massive stars 22-23
Blue supergiant star
    Hertzsprung-Russell
        diagram 19
    Stellar black hole 25
Body flap 52
Boötes
    Brightest stars 58
    Northern stars 14
    Southern stars 17
Borealis Planitia
    Mercury's North Pole 31
    Structure of Mercury 31
Bramante 31
Breathing valve 53
Brightest stars 58
Brightness standard indicator
    54
B ring 42-43
Brontë 30
Budh Planitia 31

C

3C275 (quasar) 7
Cable harness 54
Caelum 14
Calcium line 19
Callisto
    Jupiter's moons 40
    Moons 57
Caloris Basin 30-31
Caloris Montes 31
Calypso 57
Campbell 37
Canals 38
Cancer
    Northern stars 14
    Southern stars 17
Canes Venatici
    Northern stars 14
    Southern stars 17
Canis Major 17
    Brightest stars 58
    Nearest stars 58
    Northern stars 14
    Southern stars 17
Canis Minor
    Brightest stars 58
    Northern stars 14
    Southern stars 17

Canopus
    Brightest stars 58
    Our galaxy and nearby
        galaxies 11
Cap 53
Capella
    Brightest stars 58
    Northern stars 14
    Southern stars 17
Capricornus
    Northern stars 15
    Southern stars 16
Carbon
    Small stars 20-21
    Structure of red supergiant
        22
Carbon dioxide
    Earth's atmosphere 35
    Mars' atmosphere 39
    Structure of comet 49
    Venus' atmosphere 33
Carbon monoxide
    Mars' atmosphere 39
    Venus' atmosphere 33
Cargo bay 52
Caribbean plate 34
Carina
    Brightest stars 58
    Local Group of galaxies 58
    Southern stars 17
Carme 57
Cassini Division
    Saturn's rings 42
    Structure of Saturn 43
Cassiopeia 15
Castor
    Northern stars 14
    Southern stars 17
Catharina 36
Celestial equator 59
    Stars of northern skies 14-15
    Stars of southern skies 16-17
Celestial poles 59
    Stars of northern skies 14
Celestial sphere 59
    Stars of northern skies 14
Centaur 58
Centaurus
    Brightest stars 58
    Nearest stars 58
    Northern stars 14
    Southern stars 17
Centaurus and Crux 17
Centaurus A (radio galaxy) 9
Central bulge
    Galaxies 8
    Milky Way 10
Central peak
    Degas and Brontë 30
    Venus' craters 32
Cepheus 15
Ceraunius Tholus 39
Cetus
    Nearest stars 58
    Northern stars 15
    Southern stars 16
Charioteer 58
Charon 57
    Pluto 46
Chassis support bracket 54
Chekhov 31
Chi$_1$ Orionis 14
Chi$_2$ Orionis 14
Chong Ch'ol 31
Chromosphere 28-29
Chromosphere temperature
    29
Chryse Planitia 39
Cirrus cloud
    Neptune 46
    Structure of Mars 39
Clavius 36
Cleomedes 36
Cleopatra Patera 33
Cloud deck
    High-altitude clouds 46
    Structure of Neptune 47
Cloud features
    Neptune 46
    Saturn 42
    Venus 32
Clouds
    Earth 35
    Jupiter 40-41
    Mars 38-39
    Neptune 46-47
    Saturn 42-43

Uranus 44-45
Venus 32-33
Cloud shadow 46
Clouds of dust and gas
    Life of massive star 20
    Milky Way 10-11
    Nebulae and star clusters
        12-13
    Origin and expansion of
        Universe 7
    Small stars 20
Cloud-top temperature
    Structure of Jupiter 41
    Structure of Neptune 47
    Structure of Saturn 43
    Structure of Uranus 45
Cluster of galaxies 6-7
Cocos plate 34
Coleridge 31
Colette 33
Colliding galaxies 9
Columba
    Northern stars 14
    Southern stars 17
Coma 48-49
Coma Berenices
    Northern stars 14
    Southern stars 17
Comets 48-49, 59
    Famous comets 56
    Solar System 26
Comet tails 48-49
Command module 55
Communications aerial 52
Communications connector 53
Communications headset 53
Communications input socket 53
Compton 37
Congo Basin 35
Constellation 59
    Brightest stars 58
    Nearest stars 58
    Stars of northern skies 14-15
    Stars of southern skies 16-17
Control panel for PLSS 53
Convection cell 29
Convective zone
    Main sequence star 20
    Structure of Sun 29
Cooling radiator 54
Co-orbital moons 42
Copernicus 36
Coprates Chasma 39
Cor Caroli
    Northern stars 14
    Southern stars 17
Cordelia 57
Cord pull 53
Core
    Helix Nebula 13
    Massive stars 22-23
    The Moon 36
    Neutron stars and black holes
        24-25
    Small stars 20-21
    Structure of comet 49
    Structure of Jupiter 41
    Structure of Mars 39
    Structure of Mercury 31
    Structure of Neptune 47
    Structure of Pluto 47
    Structure of Saturn 43
    Structure of Uranus 45
    Structure of Venus 33
Core temperature
    Structure of Earth 35
    Structure of Jupiter 41
    Structure of main sequence
        star 20
    Structure of red giant 21
    Structure of red supergiant
        22
    Structure of Saturn 43
    Structure of Sun 29
    Structure of Uranus 45
    Sun 56
Corona 28-29
Corona Australis 15
Corona Borealis
    Northern stars 14
    Southern stars 17
Corona temperature 29
Corvus
    Northern stars 14
    Southern stars 17
Cosmic background radiation 6
Crab Nebula 24

Crater
Mercury's North Pole 31
Northern stars 14
Oceanus Procellarum 36
Southern stars 17
Surface features of Mars 38
Cressida 57
Crew handrail 50
Crew hatch 55
C ring 42-43
Crust
Far side of the Moon 37
Pulsar 24
Structure of Earth 35
Structure of Mars 39
Structure of Mercury 31
Structure of Venus 33
Crux-Centaurus Arm 10
Crystalline external crust 24
Cyclonic storm
Structure of Earth 35
Structure of Mars 39
Structure of Neptune 46
Cygnus
Northern stars 15
Southern stars 16
Cyrillus 36

D

D'Alembert 37
Danilova 32
Dark nebulae 59
Nebulae and star clusters 12
Darwin 39
Day 59
Planets 56
DDO 210 (irregular galaxy) 58
Debris 30
Declination setting circle 50
Degas 30
Deimos
Mars 38
Moons 57
Dekla Tessera 33
De la Rue 36
Delphinus
Northern stars 15
Southern stars 16
Delta Andromedae 15
Delta Crucis 17
Delta Hydri 16
Delta ring 44
Deneb
Hertzsprung-Russell diagram 19
Northern stars 15
Southern stars 16
Deneb Algedi
Northern stars 15
Southern stars 16
Deneb Kaitos
Northern stars 15
Southern stars 16
Denebola
Northern stars 14
Southern stars 17
Density
Formation of black hole 25
Massive stars 22-23
Planets 56
Small stars 20-21
Stellar black hole 25
Descent capsule 51
Descent engine 55
Descent stage 55
Desdemona 57
Desert 34
Deslandres 36
Despina 57
Deuterium nucleus 18
Diameter
Earth 26, 56
Jupiter 26, 40, 56
Jupiter's moons 40, 57
Life of massive star 22-23
Life of small star 21-22
Local Group of galaxies 58
Mars 26, 56
Mars' moons 38, 57
Mercury 26, 56
The Moon 36, 57
Moons 57
Neptune 27, 56
Neptune's moons 46, 57

Planets 26-27, 56
Pluto 27, 56
Pluto's moon 57
Saturn 27, 42, 56
Saturn's moons 42, 57
Stars 18
Sun 28, 56
Uranus 27, 44, 56
Uranus' moons 44, 57
Venus 26, 56
Dihedral mirror 54
Dione
Moons 57
Saturn's moons 42
Disc of spiral arms 10
Discovery Rupes 31
Distance 58
Doppler 37
Dorado 17
Dosimeter pocket 53
Double-planet system
Earth 34
Pluto 46
Draco
Local Group of galaxies 58
Northern stars 15
Southern stars 16
D ring 42-43
Dubhe
Northern stars 14
The Plough 15
Dust
Asteroids, comets, and meteoroids 48-49
Far side of the Moon 37
Mars 38-39
Nebulae and star clusters 12-13
NGC 2997 (spiral galaxy) 8
Overhead view of our galaxy 10
Solar System 26
Venus' atmosphere 33
Dust cloud
Large Magellanic Cloud 8
Mars 38-39
Milky Way 10-11
Nebulae and star clusters 12-13
Origin and expansion of Universe 7
Dust lane
Horsehead Nebula 12
NGC 2997 (spiral galaxy) 8
Optical image of Centaurus A 9
Rings and dust lanes 44
Trifid Nebula 12
Dust particles 49
Dust storm 39
Dust tail 48-49
Dwarf star 59

E

Earphone 53
Earth 34-35
Energy emission from Sun 18
Objects in Universe 7
Phases of the Moon 37
Planets 56
Solar eclipse 28
Solar System 26
Earthquake region 35
Earthquakes 34
Ecliptic 59
Inclination of planetary orbits 27
Stars of northern skies 14-15
Stars of southern skies 16-17
Eisila Regio
Radar map of Venus 32
Structure of Venus 33
Ejecta
Degas and Brönte 30
Features of supernova 23
Ray crater 30
Venusian craters 32
Elara 57
Electrical connector 54
Electricity line and connector 53
Electromagnetic radiation 59
Electromechanical drive unit 54

Elevon 52
Elliptical orbit 26
Elliptical galaxy 59
Galaxies 8
Local Group of galaxies 58
Objects in Universe 7
Origin and expansion of Universe 7
El Nath
Northern stars 14
Southern stars 17
Eltanin 15
Emergency oxygen feed 53
Emission nebula 59
Large Magellanic Cloud 8
Milky Way 10
Nebulae and star clusters 12-13
Objects in Universe 7
Enceladus
Moons 57
Saturn's moons 42
Encke 36
Encke Division
Saturn's rings 42
Structure of Saturn 43
Energy emission from Sun 18
Engine system propellant tank 51
Enif
Northern stars 15
Pegasus and Andromeda 15
Southern stars 16
Entrance/exit platform 55
Epimetheus 57
Epsilon Centauri 17
Epsilon Crucis 17
Epsilon Hydri 16
Epsilon ring
Structure of Uranus 45
Uranus' rings 44
Equator 43
Equatorial diameter 56
Equatorial mount 50
Equatorial rotation period 56
Equatorial Zone 41
Equipment box 50
Equipment module 52
Equuleus
Northern stars 15
Southern stars 16
Eridanus
Brightest stars 58
Northern stars 15
Southern stars 16
E ring 42
Escape velocity 56
Eta Centauri 17
Eta Mensae 16
Eta Orionis 14
Eta ring 44
Eta Sagittarii 17
Eurasian plate 34
Europa
Jupiter's moons 40
Moons 57
Europe
Satellite views of Earth 34
Structure of Earth 35
Eve 33
Event horizon 59
Neutron stars and black holes 24-25
Exhalation tube 53
Exhaust deflector 55
Extendable aerial 54
External crust 24
External tank 52
Extravehicular glove 53
Eyepiece 50
Eyepiece lens 50

F

Fabry 37
Far side of the Moon 37
Fibrils 28
Filament
Nebulae and star clusters 12-13
Sun 28-29
Final stage engine 52
Final stage of launch vehicle 52
Finder scope 50
Fireball 6
First quarter 37

Flamsteed 36
Fleming 37
Flight deck windscreen 52
Focusing knob 50
Fog 38-39
Fomalhaut
Northern stars 15
Southern stars 16
Footpad
Apollo 16 55
Viking 51
Formation of black hole 25
Formation of ray crater 30
Fornax
Local Group of galaxies 58
Northern stars 15
Southern stars 16
Fracastorius 36
Fractured rock 30
Fra Mauro 36
Fram Rupes 31
F ring 42-43
Furnerius 36
Furud 37
Fuselage skin 52
Fusion crust 48

G

Gacrux 17
Gagarin 37
Gagarin, Yuri 52
Galactic centre
Milky Way 10
Stars of northern skies 14
Stars of southern skies 16
Galactic nucleus 8-9
Galactic plane 10-11
Galatea 57
Galaxies 8-9, 59
Local Group of galaxies 58
Milky Way 10-11
Universe 6-7
Galilean moons 40
Galle ring
Neptune's rings 46
Structure of Neptune 47
Galois 37
Gamma
Northern stars 14
Southern stars 17
Gamma Centauri 17
Gamma Hydri 16
Gamma Mensae 16
Gamma radiation 6
Gamma rays 18
Gamma ring 44
Ganymede
Jupiter's moons 40
Moons 57
Gas
Asteroids, comets, and meteoroids 48-49
Massive stars 22-23
NGC 2997 (spiral galaxy) 8
Small stars 20-21
Stellar black hole 25
Gas chromatograph mass spectrometer processor 51
Gas cloud
Milky Way 10
Nebulae and star clusters 12-13
Origin and expansion of Universe 6-7
Gas current 25
Gaseous water 45
Gas giants
Jupiter 40-41
Neptune 46-47
Saturn 42-43
Solar System 26-27
Uranus 44-45
Gas loop 28-29
Gas molecules 49
Gas pressure bottle 52
Gassendi 36
Gas shell
Life of small star 21
Nebulae and star clusters 12-13
Gas tail 48-49
Gemini 14
Giant stars 59
Massive stars 22
Stars 18-19

Globular cluster
M22 (globular cluster) 17
Nebulae and star clusters 12
Objects in Universe 8
Globule
Life of massive star 22
Small stars 20
Glossary 59
Glove connector 53
Gold coating 53
Goya 31
GR 8 (irregular galaxy) 58
Graffias 17
Granulated surface
Structure of Sun 29
Sunspots 28
Grassland 34
Gravitation (gravity) 59
Neutron stars and black holes 24
Universe 6
Great Bear 58
Great Dark Spot 46-47
Great Dog 58
Great Red Spot 40-41
Greenhouse effect 32
Greenland 35
Grimaldi 36
G ring 42
Grus
Northern stars 15
Southern stars 16
Guinevere Planitia
Radar map of Venus 32
Structure of Venus 33
Gula Mons 33
Gutenberg discontinuity 35

H

Hadar
Centaurus and Crux 17
Southern stars 17
Halley's Comet 48
Halo 10
Halo ring 40
Hamal
Northern stars 15
Pegasus and Andromeda 15
Southern stars 16
Handle 53
Hathor Mons 33
Hawthorne 31
Haze
Saturn's atmosphere 43
Venus' atmosphere 33
Head 49
Headset 53
Heater reflector shield 54
Heat shield 51
Heavy chemical elements 23
Heine 31
Heka 14
Helene 57
Helen Planitia 32
Helium
Jupiter 40-41
Massive stars 22
Mercury's atmosphere 31
Neptune's atmosphere 47
Pluto's atmosphere 47
Saturn 42-43
Small stars 20-21
Sun 28
Uranus' atmosphere 45
Helium-3 nucleus 18
Helium-4 nucleus 18
Helium line 19
Helix Nebula 13
Hellenic plate 34
Helmet attachment ring 53
Hercules
Near side of the Moon 36
Northern stars 15
Southern stars 16
Herdsman 58
Herodotus 36
Hertzsprung 37
Hertzsprung-Russell diagram 59
Stars 18-19
Hestia Rupes 33
High-altitude clouds
Jupiter 41
Neptune 46

High-energy radiation 18
High-gain aerial 50
High-gain parabolic aerial 51
Hilbert 37
Himalayas 34
Himalia 57
Hinged lid 54
Holden 39
Horizontal-scan panoramic camera 54
Horsehead Nebula 12
Hot spot 25
Howe 32
Hubble Space Telescope 50
Huntsman 58
Hydra
Northern stars 14
Southern stars 17
Hydrogen
Jupiter's atmosphere 41
Massive stars 22
Mercury's atmosphere 31
Nebulae and star clusters 12-13
Neptune's atmosphere 47
Nuclear fusion in Sun 18
Saturn's atmosphere 43
Small stars 20-21
Sun 28
Uranus' atmosphere 45
Hydrogen alpha line 19
Hydrogen beta line 19
Hydrogen gamma line 19
Hydrogen nucleus 18
Hydrogen sulphide 47
Hydrus 16
Southern stars 16
Hyperion 57

I

Iapetus 57
IC 10 (irregular galaxy) 58
IC 1613 (irregular galaxy) 58
IC 5152 (irregular galaxy) 58
Ice crystals 35
Illuminator 50
Incident light ray 50
Inclination of planetary orbits to ecliptic 27
Indian Ocean 34
Indo-Australian plate 34
Indus 16
Infra-red map of our galaxy 11
Infra-red radiation
Energy emission from Sun 18
Infra-red map of our galaxy 11
Inner core
Far side of the Moon 37
Structure of Earth 35
Inner mantle
Jupiter 40-41
Saturn 42-43
Inner planetary orbits 27
Instrument bay 54
Instrument compartment
Luna 9 54
Mars 3 51
Insulation 54
Integrated thermal micrometeoroid garment 53
Internal crust 24
Io
Jupiter's moons 40
Moons 57
Iota Centauri 17
Iota Pegasi 15
Iota Sagittarii 17
Iron
Meteorites 48
Structure of Earth 35
Structure of Mercury 31
Structure of Venus 33
Iron oxide dust 38
Irregular galaxy 59
Galaxies 8
Local Group of galaxies 58
Objects in Universe 7
Origin and expansion of Universe 6-7
Our galaxy and nearby galaxies 11
Ishtar Terra 32-33

J

Janus 57
Jet of gas and dust 49
Jewel Box 7
Joliot 37
Jules Verne 37
Juliet 57
Julius Caesar 36
Jupiter 40-41
    Planets 56
    Solar System 26-27

K

Kappa Pegasi 15
Kaus Australis
    Northern stars 15
    Sagittarius 17
    Southern stars 16
Kaus Borealis 17
Kaus Meridionalis 17
Keel 58
Keeler 37
Kepler 36
Kochab 14
Korolev 37
Kuan Han-ch'ing 31

L

Lacerta
    Northern stars 15
    Southern stars 16
Lada Terra
    Radar map of Venus 32
    Structure of Venus 33
Ladder 55
Lagoon Nebula 17
Lakshmi Planum 33
Lalande 21185 58
Lambda Andromedae 15
Lambda Pegasi 15
Lampland 39
Landing leg 55
Landing shock-absorber 51
Langrenus 36
Large Magellanic Cloud
    Hydrus and Mensa 16
    Local Group of galaxies 58
    Our galaxy and nearby
    galaxies 11
    Stars of southern skies
    16-17
Larissa 57
Last quarter 37
Launch support 52
Lava flow 38
Lavinia Planitia
    Radar map of Venus 32
    Structure of Venus 33
Leading edge of wing 52
Leda 57
Leda Planitia
    Radar map of Venus 32
    Structure of Venus 33
Leibnitz 37
Leo
    Nearest stars 58
    Northern stars 14
    Southern stars 17
Leo I 58
Leo II 58
Leo A 58
Leo Minor
    Northern stars 14
    Southern stars 17
Leonid meteor shower 48
Lepus 17
Letronne 36
Le Verrier ring
    Structure of Uranus 47
    Uranus' rings 46
Liang K'ai 31
Libra
    Northern stars 14
    Southern stars 16
Life of massive star 22-23
Life of small star 20-21
Liftable visor 53
Light hour 10
Lightning 41
Light second 59
Light shield 50

Light year 59
    Milky Way 10
Line of sight 37
Lion 58
Liquid-cooled undergarment
    53
Liquid helium 41
Liquid hydrogen
    Jupiter 40-41
    Saturn 42-43
Liquid oxygen tank vent-valve
    and fairing 52
Little Dog 58
Local Arm 10
Local Group of galaxies 58, 59
Location of Solar System 10
Locking mechanism 54
Locking mechanism cable 54
Locking system 53
Looped prominence 28-29
Lowell 37
Lower-energy radiation 18
Lower haze 33
Low-gain aerial 51
Luminosity 59
    Local Group of galaxies 58
    Sun 56
Luna 9 54
Lunae Planum 39
Lunar eclipse 59
    Total lunar eclipses 57
Lunar exploration 54-55
Lunar extravehicular visor 53
Lunar Module 55
Lunar Module restraint ring 53
Lunar overshoe 53
Lunar Rover 55
Lunokhod 1 54
Lupus 14
Lynx
    Northern stars 14
    Southern stars 17
Lyra
    Brightest stars 58
    Northern stars 15
    Southern stars 16
Lyre 58
Lysithea 57

M

M22 (globular cluster) 17
M31 (spiral galaxy) 58
M32 (elliptical galaxy) 58
M33 (spiral galaxy) 58
Mach 37
Macrobius 36
Macrospicule 29
Magellanic Cloud
    Hydrus and Mensa 16
    Local Group of galaxies 58
    Our galaxy and nearby
    galaxies 11
    Stars of southern skies 16
Maginus 36
Magnesium lines 19
Magnetic axis 24
Magnetic field line 24
Magnetometer 51
Magnifying mirror 51
Magnitude 59
    Brightest stars 58
    Nearest stars 58
    Stars 18
    Sun 56
Main engines 52
Main ring 40
Main sequence star
    Massive stars 22
    Objects in Universe 7
    Small stars 20
    Stars 18-19
Manned space exploration
    52-53
Manoeuvring engine 52
Mantle
    Far side of the Moon 37
    Structure of Earth 35
    Structure of Mercury 31
    Structure of Neptune 47
    Structure of Pluto 47
    Structure of Uranus 45
    Structure of Venus 33
Mare Crisium 36
Mare Fecunditatis 36

Mare Frigoris 36
Mare Humorum 36
Mare Imbrium 36
Mare Ingenii 37
Mare Moscoviense 37
Mare Nectaris 36
Mare Nubium 36
Mare Orientale 37
Mareotis Fossae 39
Mare Serenitatis 36
Mare Smithii 37
Mare Tranquillitatis 36
Mare Vaporum 36
Margaritifer Sinus 39
Maria 36
Markab
    Northern stars 15
    Pegasus and Andromeda
    15
    Southern stars 16
Markeb 17
Mars 38-39
    Planets 56
    Solar System 26
Mars 3 orbiter and lander 51
Mass
    Earth 26, 56
    Jupiter 26, 40, 56
    Mars 26, 56
    Mercury 26, 56
    Neptune 27, 56
    Planets 26-27, 56
    Pluto 27, 56
    Saturn 27, 56
    Stars 18
    Sun 56
    Uranus 27, 56
    Venus 26, 56
Massive stars 22-23
Matar 15
Maxwell Montes
    Radar map of Venus 32
    Structure of Venus 33
Megrez 15
Mendel 37
Mendeleev 37
Menkalinan 17
Menkar
    Northern stars 15
    Southern stars 16
Menkent 17
Mensa
    Southern stars 17
Merak 15
Mercury 30-31
    Planets 56
    Solar System 26
Mersenius 36
Mesospicule 35
Meteor 59
    Asteroids, comets, and
    meteoroids 48
Meteorite 59
    Asteroids, comets, and
    meteoroids 48
    Earth 34
    Far side of the Moon 37
    Ray crater 30
Meteorite impact
    Mercury 30
    The Moon 36
Meteoroids 48-49, 59
    Solar System 26
Meteorology boom assembly
    51
Meteorology sensor equipment
    51
Meteor showers 59
    Asteroids, comets, and
    meteoroids 48
    Earth's atmosphere 35
Methane
    Jupiter's atmosphere 41
    Neptune and Pluto 46-47
    Saturn's atmosphere 43
    Uranus 44-45
Methane cirrus clouds 46-47
Metis 57
Metis Regio 32
Miaplacidus 17
Michelangelo 31
Microwave map of cosmic
    background radiation 6
Microwave radiation 6
Mid-Atlantic ridge 34
Mid-Indian Ocean ridge 34
Mid-latitude band 32

Milankovic 39
Milky Way 10-11, 59
    Local Group of galaxies 58
    Northern stars 14
    Solar System 26
    Stars of southern skies 16
Milne 37
Milton 31
Mimas
    Moons 57
    Saturn's moons 42
Mimosa 17
Minor planet 59
Mintaka 14
Mira
    Northern stars 15
    Southern stars 16
Mirach
    Northern stars 15
    Pegasus and Andromeda
    15
    Southern stars 16
Miranda
    Moons 57
    Uranus' moons 44
Mirfak
    Northern stars 15
    Southern stars 16
Mirror 53
Mirzam
    Canis Major 17
    Northern stars 14
    Southern stars 17
Mizar 15
Mohorovicic discontinuity 35
Monoceros
    Northern stars 14
    Southern stars 17
Montes Apenninus 36
Montes Cordillera 37
Montes Jura 36
Montes Rook 37
Monteverdi 31
The Moon 36-37, 59
    Lunar eclipse 57, 59
    Objects in Universe 7
    Solar eclipse 28
Moonquake region 37
Moons 57, 59
    Jupiter's moons 40
    Mars' moons 38
    Neptune's moons 46
    Saturn's moons 42
    Solar System 26
    Uranus' moons 44
Moulded fingertip 53
Mountain ring 30
Mu Andromedae 15
Muliphen 17
Multilayered spacesuit 53
Mu Orionis 14
Mu Pegasi 15

N

Naiad 57
Nair Al Zaurak
    Northern stars 15
    Southern stars 16
Narrow-beam directional
    aerial 54
Nash 17
Natal cocoon
    Life of massive star 22
    Life of small star 20
Natural satellites 59
    The Moon 36
Navigation system 51
Navka 33
Nazca plate 34
Nearest stars 58
Near side of the Moon 36
Nebulae 12-13, 59
    Galaxies 8-9
    Life of massive star 22
    Milky Way 10-11
    NGC 1566 (Seyfert galaxy) 9
    Small stars 20
    Structure of nebula 20
Neck ring 53
Nefertiti Corona 33
Neon 31
Neptune 46-47
    Planets 56
    Solar System 27
Nereid 57

Neutrino 59
    Energy emission from Sun
    18
Neutron
    Neutron stars and black
    holes 24
    Nuclear fusion in Sun 18
Neutron-rich internal crust 24
Neutron stars 24-25, 59
    Massive stars 22-23
New Moon 37
NGC 147 (elliptical galaxy) 58
NGC 185 (elliptical galaxy) 58
NGC 205 (elliptical galaxy) 58
NGC 221 (elliptical galaxy) 58
NGC 1566 (Seyfert galaxy) 9
NGC 2997 (spiral galaxy) 8
NGC 4406 (elliptical galaxy) 7
NGC 4486 (elliptical galaxy) 7
NGC 5236 (spiral galaxy) 7
NGC 5754 (colliding galaxies)
    9
NGC 6656 (globular cluster) 17
NGC 6822 (irregular galaxy)
    Local Group of galaxies 58
    Objects in Universe 7
Nickel
    Structure of Earth 35
    Structure of Venus 33
Niobe Planitia
    Radar map of Venus 32
    Structure of Venus 33
Nitrogen
    Earth's atmosphere 35
    Helix Nebula 13
    Mars' atmosphere 39
    Pluto's atmosphere 47
    Venus' atmosphere 33
Noctis Labryrinthus 38
    Structure of Mars 39
North America 34
North American plate 34
North Equatorial Belt 41
North Galactic Pole 11
North Galactic spur 11
North magnetic polar region
    24
North polar aurora 41
North polar ice-cap
    Structure of Earth 34
    Structure of Mars 39
North Pole
    Earth 34
    Jupiter 40
    Mars 38
    Mercury 30
    The Moon 36
    Neptune 46
    Pluto 47
    Pulsar 24
    Saturn 42
    Uranus 44
    Venus 32
North Temperate Belt 41
North Temperate Zone 41
North Tropical Zone 41
Nose containing air-data
    computer 52
Nose fairing 52
Nozzle and thrust vector
    control system 52
Nu Andromedae 15
Nuclear fusion
    Massive stars 22
    Small stars 20
    Stars 18
    Sun 28
Nuclear-powered heater 54
Nucleus
    Asteroids, comets, and
    meteoroids 48-49
    Galaxies 8- 9
    Overhead view of our galaxy
    10
    Side view of our galaxy 10
Nunki
    Northern stars 15
    Sagittarius 17
    Southern stars 16
Nu Orionis 14

O

Oberon
    Moons 57
    Uranus' moons 44

Objective lens 50
Objective lens cell 50
Observing space 50-51
Oceans 34-35
Oceanus Procellarum 36
Olivine 48
Olympus Mons 38-39
Omega Centauri 17
Omicron Andromedae 15
Omicron Orionis 14
Omicron₁ Canis Majoris 17
Omicron₂ Canis Majoris 17
Omicron Orionis 14
Omicron Sagittarii 17
Oort Cloud 48
Open cluster 12
Ophelia 57
Ophiuchus
    Nearest stars 58
    Northern stars 15
    Southern stars 16
Optical map of our galaxy
    10-11
Orbit 59
    Inner planetary orbits 26
    Outer planetary orbits 27
    Stars of northern skies 14
    Stars of southern skies 16
Orbital motion
    Comet tails 48
    Orbits of outer planets 27
Orbital path of the Moon 37
Orbital period 59
    Moons 57
    Planets 56
Orbital plane 59
    Earth 34
    Jupiter 40
    Mars 38
    Mercury 30
    The Moon 36
    Neptune 46
    Pluto 47
    Saturn 42
    Uranus 44
    Venus 32
Orbital speed (velocity)
    Mercury 30
    Planets 56
    Solar System 26-27
Orbital tilt 59
    Moons 57
    Planets 56
Orion
    Brightest stars 58
    Northern stars 14
    Southern stars 17
    Star formation in Orion
    20
Orion Arm 10
Orion Nebula 13
    Orion 14
    Our galaxy and nearby
    galaxies 11
Orion's belt
    Horsehead Nebula 12
    Orion 14
    Our galaxy and nearby
    galaxies 11
"Orlan D" spacesuit 53
Outer core
    Far side of the Moon 37
    Structure of Earth 35
Outer envelope
    Structure of red giant 21
    Structure of red supergiant
    22
Outer mantle
    Jupiter 40-41
    Saturn 42-43
Oval
    Cloud features of Saturn 42
    Structure of Saturn 43
Ovda Regio
    Radar map of Venus 32
    Structure of Venus 33
Overhead view of our galaxy
    10
Oversuit 53
Oxygen
    Earth's atmosphere 35
    Helix Nebula 13
    Mars' atmosphere 39
    Mercury's atmosphere 31
    Structure of red supergiant
    22
Oxygen inlet and outlet 53
Ozone layer 35

P

Pacific-Antarctic rise 34
Pacific Ocean 34
Pacific plate 34
Pan 57
Pandora 57
Panoramic infra-red map of
  our galaxy 11
Panoramic optical map of our
  galaxy and nearby galaxies
  10-11
Panoramic radio map of our
  galaxy 11
Parabolic aerial 51
Parachute container 51
Parsec 59
Partial solar eclipse 28
Particle radiation 59
Pasiphae 57
Pasteur 37
Pavlova 33
Pavo 16
Pavonis Mons 39
Peacock 16
Pegasus 15
  Local Group of galaxies
  58
  Northern stars 15
  Southern stars 16
Pegasus and Andromeda 15
Penlight pocket 53
Penumbra
  Solar eclipse 28
  Sunspots 28
Perigee 59
Perihelion 59
  Planets 26-27, 56
Perpendicular to orbital plane
  Earth 54
  Jupiter 40
  Mars 38
  Mercury 30
  The Moon 36
  Neptune 46
  Pluto 47
  Saturn 42
  Uranus 44
  Venus 32
Perseus
  Northern stars 15
  Southern stars 16
Perseus Arm 10-11
Petavius 36
Phaet 17
Phases 59
Phases of the Moon 37
Phekda 15
Phi Andromedae 15
Phidias 31
Philippine plate 34
Philoxenus 31
Phobos
  Mars 38
  Moons 57
Phoebe 57
Phoebe Regio 32
Phoenix
  Northern stars 15
  Southern stars 16
Photosphere 28-29
Photosphere temperature
  Structure of Sun 29
  Surface features of Sun 28
Pi Canis Majoris 17
Pictor 17
Pincers 53
Pi_2 Orionis 14
Pi_3 Orionis 14
Pi_4 Orionis 14
Pi_5 Orionis 14
Pi_6 Orionis 14
Pi Pegasi 15
Pi Sagittarii 17
Pisces
  Local Group of galaxies 58
  Northern stars 15
  Southern stars 16
Pisces Austrinus
  Northern stars 15
  Southern stars 16
Pitatus 36
Pitch and yaw control engine
  52
Planck 37
Planet 59

Planetary nebula
  Nebulae and star clusters 13
  Small stars 20-21
Planetary orbits 26-27
Planetary rotation 26
Planets 56
  Earth 34-35
  Jupiter 40-41
  Mars 38-39
  Mercury 30-31
  Neptune 46-47
  Pluto 46-47
  Saturn 42-43
  Solar System 26-27
  Uranus 44-45
  Venus 32-33
Plateau
  Neptune's rings 46
  Structure of Neptune 47
Plato 36
Pleiades 12
  Northern stars 15
  Our galaxy and nearby
  galaxies 10
  Southern stars 16
The Plough 15
PLSS 52-53
Plume 41
Pluto 46-47
  Moons 57
  Planets 56
  Solar System 27
Polar axis scope 50
Polar band 32
Polar hood 32
Polaris
  Our galaxy and nearby
  galaxies 10
  Stars of northern skies 14-15
Polar rotation period 56
Pole star
  Our galaxy and nearby
  galaxies 10
  Stars of northern skies 14
Pollux
  Northern stars 14
  Southern stars 17
Polygnotus 31
Porrima 17
Portable life-support system
  52-53
Portia 57
Positron 18
Potassium 31
Praesepe 14
Praxiteles 31
Pressure
  Formation of black hole 25
  Stellar black hole 25
Pressure bottle 51
Pressure glove 53
Pressure helmet 53
Pressure indicator 53
Pressure mode selector 53
Pressure relief valve 53
Primary mirror 50
Primary mirror housing 50
Primary shock-absorber strut
  55
Procyon
  Brightest stars 58
  Northern stars 14
  Southern stars 17
Prometheus 57
Prominence 28-29
Proteus
  Moons 57
  Neptune's moons 46
Protogalaxies 6-7
Proton 18
Protostar 59
  Life of massive star 22
  Small stars 20
Proxima Centauri
  Nearest stars 58
  Stars of northern skies 14
Psi Sagittarii 17
Ptolemaeus 36
Puck 57
Pulsar 59
  Neutron stars and black
  holes 24
Puppis
  Northern stars 14
  Southern stars 17
Pyroxene 48
Pyxis 14

Q

Quasar nucleus 9
Quasar (quasi-stellar object) 59
  Galaxies 8
  Objects in Universe 7
  Origin and expansion of
  Universe 6-7

R

Radar map of Venus 32
Radial spoke 43
Radiation 59
  Earth 34
  Energy emission from Sun
  18
  Galaxies 8-9
  Nebulae and star clusters 12
  Observing space 50
  Universe 6
Radiative zone
  Structure of main sequence
  star 20
  Structure of Sun 29
Radiator
  Lunokhod 1 54
  Mars 3 51
  Vostok 1 52
Radio command link aerial 52
Radio galaxies 8-9
Radio image
  3C273 (quasar) 9
  Centaurus A 9
Radio lobe 9
Radio map of our galaxy 11
Radio pocket 53
Radio telescope 50
Radio wave beam 24
Radio-wave emission 11
Radio waves
  Pulsar 24
  Radio image of Centaurus A
  9
Radio whip aerial 52
Ras Algethi 16
Ras Alhague
  Northern stars 15
  Southern stars 16
Ray
  Mercury 30
  Near side of the Moon 36
Ray crater 30
Reaction control engine 52
Reaction control thruster 55
Red dwarf 59
  Hertzsprung-Russell
  diagram 19
Red giant
  Small stars 20-21
  Stars 18-19
Red spot 40-41
Red supergiant
  Massive stars 22-23
  Stars 18-19
Re-entry module 52
Reflected light ray 50
Reflection nebula 59
  Nebulae and star clusters 12
Reflector 50
Refracted light ray 50
Refractor telescope 50
Regolith (soil) 37
Regulus
  Northern stars 14
  Southern stars 17
Rendezvous radar 55
Renoir 31
Research apparatus aerial 51
Retaining strap 53
Reticulum 16
Retrograde motion 59
Reverse shock wave 23
Rhea 57
Rho_1 Sagittarii 17
Rigel
  Brightest stars 58
  Northern stars 14
  Orion 14
  Southern stars 17
  Star magnitudes 18
Right ascension setting circle
  50
Ring 6 44
Ring 1986 U1R 44

Ring 1986 U2R 44
Rings 56
  Jupiter's rings 40-41
  Neptune's rings 46-47
  Planets 56
  Saturn's rings 42-43
  Uranus' rings 44-45
Rings 4 and 5 44
Ring system 59
Ritchey 39
River Eridanus 58
Roche 37
Rock 30
Rocky planets
  Earth 35-36
  Mars 38-39
  Mercury 30-31
  Solar System 26-27
  Venus 32-33
Roll engine 51
Rosalind 57
Rosette Nebula 7
Rotational period
  Planets 56
  Sun 56
  Venus 32
Rubens 31
Rudder and speed brake 52
Rupes 30
Rupes Altai 36

S

62 Sagittarii 17
Sabik 16
Sacajawea 33
Sagitta 16
Sagittarius 17
  Local Group of galaxies 58
  Northern stars 15
  Southern stars 16
Sagittarius Arm 10
Sahara
  Satellite views of Earth 34
  Structure of Earth 35
Saiph 14
Sampler head 51
Sappho Patera 33
Satellite 59
  Observing space 50-51
Satellite views of Earth 34
Saturn 42-43
  Moons 57
  Planets 56
  Solar System 27
S-band high-gain aerial 51
S-band low-gain aerial 51
S-band steerable aerial 55
Scheat
  Northern stars 15
  Pegasus and Andromeda 15
  Southern stars 16
Schedar 15
Schickard 36
Schrödinger 37
Schubert 31
Scooter 46-47
Scorpius
  Northern stars 15
  Southern stars 16
Scrubland 34
Sculptor
  Local Group of galaxies 58
  Northern stars 15
  Southern stars 16
Scutum 15
Secondary crater 30
Secondary mirror 50
Secondary shock-absorber
  strut 55
Securing band 52
Securing strap 53
Security line 53
Sedna Planitia
  Radar map of Venus 32
  Structure of Venus 33
Semi-solid core 33
Semi-solid outer core 37
Serpens Caput
  Northern stars 14
  Southern stars 17
Serpens Cauda
  Northern stars 15
  Southern stars 16
Serpent Bearer 58
Service module 55

Seven Sisters 10
Sextans
  Local Group of galaxies 58
  Southern stars 17
Seyfert 37
Seyfert galaxies 8-9
Shaula
  Northern stars 15
  Southern stars 16
Shell
  Hubble Space Telescope 50
  Massive stars 22
  Small stars 20-21
Shelley 31
Shield volcano 38
Shock-absorber 51
Shock-absorber strut 55
Shock wave 23
Shrubland 34
Side hatch 52
Sidereal day 59
Sidereal year 59
Side view of our galaxy 10
Sif Mons 33
Sigma Canis Majoris 17
Silicate core 47
Silicate dust 49
Silicate material 35
Silicon 22
Singularity 59
  Formation of black hole 25
  Stellar black hole 25
Sinope 57
Sinus Iridum 36
Sirius
  Canis Major 17
  Northern stars 14
  Our galaxy and nearby
  galaxies 11
  Southern stars 17
  Spectral absorption lines 19
  Star magnitudes 18
Sirius A
  Brightest stars 58
  Hertzsprung-Russell
  diagram 19
  Nearest stars 58
Sirius B
  Hertzsprung-Russell
  diagram 19
  Nearest stars 58
Skirt 52
Slipher 59
Small Dark Spot 46-47
Small Magellanic Cloud
  Hydrus and Mensa 16
  Local Group of galaxies 58
  Our galaxy and nearby
  galaxies 11
  Stars of southern skies 16
Small stars 20-21
Snap-on fastening 53
Sodium 31
Sodium lines 19
Solar day 59
  Mercury 30
Solar eclipse 28, 57, 59
Solar flare 28-29
Solar panel
  Hubble Space Telescope 50
  Lunokhod 1 54
  Mars 3 51
Solar panel drive 54
Solar System 26-27, 59
Solar wind
  Structure of comet 49
  Sun 28
Solid rocket booster 52
Sombrero 8
Sophocles 31
Sobkou Planitia 31
South America
  Satellite views of Earth 34
  Structure of Earth 35
South American plate 34
South Atlantic Ocean 35
South Equatorial Belt 41
South Galactic Pole 11
South magnetic polar region 24
South Pacific Ocean 35
South polar ice-cap
  Structure of Mars 39
  Surface of Mars 38
South Pole
  Earth 34
  Jupiter 40
  Mars 38

Mercury 30
The Moon 36
Neptune 46
Pluto 47
Pulsar 24
Saturn 42
Uranus 44-45
Venus 32
South Temperate Belt 41
South Temperate Zone 41
South Tropical Zone 41
Space Shuttle 52
Spacesuits 53
Spectral absorption lines 18-19
Spectral type 18-19
Spectrum 59
Spica
  Northern stars 14
  Southern stars 17
Spicule
  Structure of Sun 29
  Surface of Sun 28
Spiral arm
  Galaxies 8-9
  Milky Way 10
Spiral galaxy 59
  Galaxies 8-9
  Local Group of galaxies 58
  Milky Way 10-11
  Objects in Universe 7
  Origin and expansion of
  Universe 6-7
Spirit level 50
Spoke 54
Starbirth region 12
Star clusters 12-13
  Objects in Universe 7
  Our galaxy and nearby
  galaxies 10
Star diagonal 50
Star formation in Orion 20
Star magnitudes 18
Stars 18-19, 59
  Brightest stars 58
  Massive stars 22-23
  Milky Way 10-11
  Nearest stars 58
  Neutron stars and black
  holes 24-25
  Small stars 20-21
  Star clusters 12
  Sun 28-29
Stars of northern skies 14-15
Stars of southern skies 16-17
Star type
  Brightest stars 58
  Nearest stars 58
  Sun 56
Stellar black hole 25
Stellar core
  Formation of black hole 25
  Helix Nebula 13
Stellar spectral absorption lines
  18-19
Stöfler 36
Stony-iron meteorite 48
Stony meteorite 48
Stratosphere
  Earth's atmosphere 35
  Jupiter's atmosphere 41
  Mars' atmosphere 39
  Saturn's atmosphere 43
Striation 42
Strindberg 31
Suit fastener 53
Sulphur dioxide 33
Sulphuric acid 32-33
Summit caldera 38
Sun 28-29, 59
  Brightest stars 58
  Comet tails 48
  Energy emission from Sun
  18
  Milky Way 10
  Nearest stars 58
  Objects in Universe 7
  Solar eclipse 28, 57, 59
  Solar System 26-27
  Stars 18-19
Sunglasses pocket 53
Sunspots 28-29
Superclusters 6
Superfluid neutrons 24
Supergiant stars 59
  Massive stars 22
  Stars 18-19
  Stellar black hole 25

Supergranule 29
Supernova 59
  Massive stars 22-23
  Nebulae and star clusters 12
  Neutron stars and black
  holes 25
Supernova remnant 59
  Nebulae and star clusters
  12-13
  X-ray image of Crab Nebula
  24
Surface contact probe 55
Surface features
  Mars 38
  Sun 28
Surface gravity 56
Surface sampler boom 51
Surface temperature
  Planets 56
  Stars 18
  Structure of Earth 35
  Structure of main sequence
  star 20
  Structure of Mars 39
  Structure of Mercury 31
  Structure of Neptune 47
  Structure of red giant 21
  Structure of red supergiant
  22
  Structure of Venus 33
  Sun 29
Syria Planum
  Structure of Mars 39
  Surface features of Mars 38

T

Tantalus Fossae 39
Tarantula Nebula 22-23
  Large Magellanic Cloud 8
Tau Orionis 14
Taurus
  Northern stars 15
  Southern stars 16
Tau Sagittarii 17
Telemetry aerial 52
Telescopes 50
Telescope tube 50
Telesto 57
Television camera
  Luna 9 54
  Lunokhod 1 54
  Viking 51

Tellus Regio
  Radar map of Venus 32
  Structure of Venus 33
Tellus Tessera 33
Tempe Fossae 39
Temperature
  Formation of black hole 25
  Planets 56
  Stellar black hole 25
Terminal descent engine 51
Terminal descent propellant
  tank 51
Tethus Regio 32
Tethys
  Moons 57
  Saturn's moons 42
Thalassa 57
Tharsis Tholus 39
Thaumasia Fossae 39
Thebe 57
Themis Regio 32
Thermal insulation 55
Thermosphere
  Earth's atmosphere 35
  Mars' atmosphere 39
  Venus' atmosphere 33
Theta Andromedae 15
Theta Pegasi 15
Theta, Sagittarii 17
Thetis Regio 32
Tilt and rotation
  Earth 34
  Jupiter 40
  Mars 38
  Mercury 30
  The Moon 36
  Neptune 46
  Pluto 47
  Saturn 42
  Uranus 44
  Venus 32
Tinatin Planitia 33
Tinted visor 53
Titan 57
Titania
  Moons 57
  Uranus' moons 44
Titanium soil grip 54
Tolstoj 31
Topography of Earth's crust 34
Total lunar eclipse 57
Total solar eclipse 28, 57
Tracking light 55
Trapezium 13

Triangulum
  Local Group of galaxies
  58
  Northern stars 15
  Southern stars 16
Triangulum Australe 17
Trifid Nebula 12
Trilobate aerial 54
Tripod 50
Tripod brace 50
Triton
  Moons 57
  Neptune's moons 46
Tropical rainforest
  Satellite views of Earth 34
  Structure of Earth 35
Tropical year 59
Troposphere
  Earth's atmosphere 35
  Jupiter's atmosphere 41
  Mars' atmosphere 39
  Saturn's atmosphere 43
  Venus' atmosphere 33
Tsiolkovsky 37
Tundra 34
Tyagaraja 31
Tycho 36

U

UHF aerial 51
Ultraviolet radiation 18
Umbra
  Solar eclipse 28
  Sunspots 28
Umbriel
  Moons 57
  Uranus' moons 44
Universe 6-7
Unmapped region
  Degas and Brontë 30
  Structure of Mercury 31
Unukalhai 17
Upper hatch 55
Upsilon Sagittarii 17
Uranius Tholus 39
Uranus 44-45
  Planets 56
  Solar System 27
Urine transfer connection 53
Ursa Major 15
  Nearest stars 58
  Northern stars 14

Ursa Minor
  Local Group of galaxies 58
  Northern stars 14
  Southern stars 17
UV Ceti A 58

V

Valles Marineris 39
Välmiki 31
Van de Graaff 37
Van Eyck 31
Variable star 59
Vastitas Borealis 39
Vega
  Brightest stars 58
  Northern stars 15
  Our galaxy and nearby
  galaxies 11
  Southern stars 16
Vela
  Northern stars 14
  Southern stars 17
Vela Supernova Remnant 13
Vendelinus 36
Vent pad 53
Venus 32-33
  Planets 56
  Solar System 26
Venus' craters 32
Vertical fin 52
Vertical-scan panoramic
  camera 54
Vesta Rupes 33
VHF aerial
  Apollo 16 55
  Vostok 1 52
Viking lander and orbiter 51
Virgo
  Northern stars 14
  Southern stars 17
Visor 53
Vivaldi 31
Volans 17
Volcanic lava
  Jupiter 40
  Mars 38
  The Moon 36
  Venus 32
Volcano
  Jupiter 40
  Mars 38
  Venus 32

Von Kármàn 37
Vostok 1 52
Vostok spacesuit 53
Voyager 2 51
Vulpecula 15
Vyāsa 31

W

Wagner 31
Walter 36
Waning crescent Moon 37
Waning gibbous Moon 37
Water
  Earth 34
  Mars 38
Water droplets 41
Water ice
  Jupiter's atmosphere 41
  Mercury's atmosphere 43
  Structure of Mars 39
  Structure of Neptune 47
Water-ice fog 38
Water-ice permafrost 39
Water inlet and outlet 53
Water vapour
  Earth's atmosphere 35
  Jupiter's atmosphere 41
  Mars' atmosphere 39
  Saturn's atmosphere 43
  Venus' atmosphere 33
Waxing crescent Moon 37
Waxing gibbous Moon 37
Wezen
  Canis Major 17
  Northern stars 14
Whale 58
Wheel 54
Wheel rim 54
White dwarfs 59
  Small stars 20-21
  Stars 18-19
White oval
  Jupiter 40-41
  Saturn 42
Wiener 37
Wind cover of radioisotope
  thermoelectric generator 51
Window 55
WLM (irregular galaxy) 58
Wolf 359 58
Wrist clamp 53

X

Xi Orionis 14
Xi Pegasi 15
Xi, Sagittarii 17
X-ray emission 24
X-ray image of Crab Nebula 24
X-ray spectrometer soil-
  analyser 54
X-ray telescope 54

Y

Year 59
  Earth 26, 56
  Jupiter 26, 56
  Mars 26, 56
  Mercury 26, 30, 56
  Neptune 27, 56
  Planets 26-27, 56
  Pluto 27, 56
  Saturn 27, 56
  Uranus 27, 56
  Venus 26, 56

Z

Zeami 31
Zeeman 37
Zeta Centauri 17
Zeta Sagittarii 17
Zone
  Jupiter 40-41
  Structure of Saturn 43
Zubenelgenubi
  Northern stars 14
  Southern stars 17
Zubeneschamali
  Northern stars 14
  Southern stars 17

Acknowledgments

Dorling Kindersley would like to thank:
John Becklake; the Memorial Museum of Cosmonautics, Moscow; the
Cosmos Pavilion, Moscow; the U.S. Space and Rocket Center, Alabama;
Broadhurst, Clarkson & Fuller Ltd

Special thanks to Susannah Massey (shoot-coordinator and translator)
and to Gevorkyan Tatyana Alekseyevna, Leading Scientific Fellow and
Historian of Cosmonautics (technical expert)

Picture research:
Catherine O'Rourke, Anna Lord

Picture credits:
The Planetarium, Armagh/Anglo-Australian Telescope Board 7car, 7cl,
7cbl, 8tr, 8b, 9tl, 9bl, 10tl, 12b, 13t, 13bl, 18tl; D. Malin 12tl, 22tr, 23tl;
ESA/PLV 7bl; NASA/JPL 5cr, 7br, 26t, 26bl, 26br, 27bl, 30t, 36tl, 36cr, 40cr,
42crb, 44tr, 46bc, 48cr, 55bc, 55br, 55bl; NASA 40tl; Royal Observatory,
Edinburgh/D. Malin 7tl, 7cr, 8c, 12cl, 12cr, 13br; Tom Van Sant/Geosphere

Project, Santa Monica/Science Photo Library 34 cl, 34cr; Duncan Brown 2l,
52b; Geoff Dann 51b; Jet Propulsion Laboratory 7cbr, 26bc, 27bc, 27bcr, 34tl,
38crb, 40cb, 40cbr, 40bc, 40br, 42tl, 42cr, 42cb, 42bc, 42br, 46tl, 46cra, 46cl,
46c, 46cr, 46br, 51tr, 51cr, 52tl, 54tl; The Lund Observatory 11b; National
Optical Astro Observatory 48tr; Science Photo Library 6bl, 24t; Jodrell Bank
2cr, 7tr, 9c; Hale Observatories 28br; Dr. William C. Keel 9br; Denis Milon
48bl; NASA 7cal, 8tl, 11tr, 26c, 27br, 28t, 30cr, 31tl, 32tl, 32cr, 32cl, 32b, 38cr,
38br, 48tl; NASA/AUI 9tr; Novosti Press Agency 38bc; David Parker 50tl; Max
Planck Institute for Radio Astronomy 11tl; Rev. Ronald Royer 28cr; US
Geological Survey/Science Photo Library 3, 26bcr, 38tl, 38bl; Floor of the
Oceans, by Bruce C. Heezen and Marie Tharp 1975. © Marie Tharp 1980.
Reproduced by permission of Marie Tharp, 1 Washington Ave, South Nyack,
NY 10960, USA 34b. **Jacket:** The Planetarium, Armagh/Anglo-Australian
Telescope Board; NASA/JPL; Jet Propulsion Laboratory; Science Photo
Library/NASA; Max Planck Institute for Radio Astronomy; US Geological
Survey
(t=top, b=bottom, a=above, l=left, r=right, c=centre)